SIXTY REASONS WHY CHRISTIAN PARENTS SHOULD SEND THEIR CHILDREN TO CHRISTIAN SCHOOLS

WHAT DIFFERENCE DOES IT MAKE?

Revised January 28, 2019

Gene Keith

Christians built the first schools and colleges in America, and there was a time when Americans were the best educated people in the world. This is no longer true. We are now living in the most illiterate period in American History. This book was written to explain the reason why and to provide the only intelligent solution. Gene Keith - gk122532@gmail.com

1

FORWARD

Christians built the first schools and colleges in America, and there was a time when Americans were the best educated people in the world. This is no longer true. We now are living in the most illiterate period in American history. In fact, American farmers of the eighteenth and nineteenth centuries were better educated than some of our college graduates of today.

The school system which we commonly call the public-school system was imported from Prussia in the 1800's by politicians Horace Mann and Edward Everett. Both men were devout humanists, and their objective was to move the schools out of the churches and get them under the ownership and control of the government like the schools they had seen in Prussia.

This Prussian School model was first introduced into the schools of Massachusetts and from there it spread to other states. Today, this Prussian, government controlled, secular, anti-Christian education model has totally replaced the original American Christian school system.

If there is any question in your mind about the real purpose of government schools. please consider the remarks of Chester Pierce, Professor of Educational Psychiatry at Harvard University, given at a Childhood Education Seminar in 1973.

"**Every child in America entering school at the age of five is mentally ill, because he comes to school with certain allegiances toward our founding fathers, toward our elected officials, toward his parents, toward a belief in a supernatural Being, toward the sovereignty of this nation as a separate entity. It's up to you teachers to make all of these sick children well by creating the International child of the future.**"

The philosophy of a truly Christian School is Biblical Theism. The philosophy of every public school in America is humanism. No teacher can change this. No principal can change this. No school board can change this. Consider the following quote.

"**The battle for mankind's future must be waged and won in the public-school classroom by teachers who correctly perceive their role as the proselytizers of a new faith. The classroom must and will become an arena of conflict between the old and the new. . . .the rotting corpse of Christianity and the new faith of Humanism.**" (**Humanist, page 26 of the January/February 1983 issue**).

We are convinced that parents who want their children to be indoctrinated in secular humanism should send them to public schools. Parents who want their children to receive a true education and not be indoctrinated in secular humanism must send them to Christian schools or teach them at home. There are no other options!

Gene Keith - gk122532@gmail.com

TABLE OF CONTENTS

CHAPTER 1

The First Schools in America were Christian Schools

The first thing we want our readers to understand is that Christians built the educational system in America. When our ancestors came to these shores, one of the first things they did was to establish churches for worship and schools for the education of their children.

Church Schools

The first schools in America met in the churches, the pastors were the teachers, and the first textbook was the Bible. As early as 1642, schools were required by law in Massachusetts. By 1650 schools were required by law in Connecticut.

First Textbooks

All of the books used in elementary education during the first century of colonial life were religious in nature. The *New England Primer* was the school-book for the masses for generations, and the most popular book in the colonies. The *New England Primer* was a Bible primer.

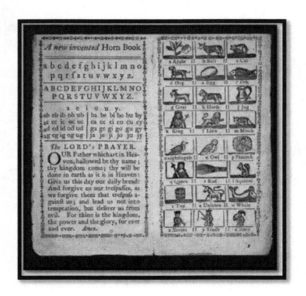

This was the book from which students learned the alphabet, reading, and writing for the first one hundred years of American History. The four most popular books were the New England Primer, the McGuffy Reader, the old blue-back spelling book, and the Noah Webster's Dictionary.

Noah Webster

Noah Webster was a born-again Christian and he considered education useless without the Bible.

Public Schools in 1950

As recently as 1950, all public-school teachers in Florida were required by law to encourage the students to practice every Christian virtue.

"To labour faithfully and earnestly for the advancement of the pupils in their studies, deportment, and morals and to embrace every opportunity to inculcate by precept and example the principles of truth, honesty, and patriotism, and the practice of every Christian virtue." *(Thomas Bailey, Trails in Florida Education, Tallahassee: 1963, page 103.).*

Public Schools in 1958

As late as 1958, Florida's public schools still acknowledged America's moral values and their religious roots. Consider the opinion of the highest-ranking public school official in Florida in 1958.

"Without God, of course, there could be no American form of government or any American way of life. Recognition of the Supreme Being is the first and most basic expression of Americanism. This, the founding fathers saw it, and thus with God's help it will continue to be." *(Thomas Bailey, Trails in Florida Education, Tallahassee: 1963, page 103.)*

In an address given on October 29, 1958, Thomas Bailey, the highest-ranking official in Florida's public schools made these remarks in an address:

"For our schools to be silent about these moral and spiritual values as related to our religious background may be, in effect, to

make our public schools an anti-religious factor in the community."

Memories

When I was growing up in Tarpon Springs, Florida, I learned more Christmas songs in our public school than I learned in our church. Our High School Chorus presented public concerts during which we sang Christian songs like, *"Go tell it on the Mountain, O Holy Night, O Come all ye Faithful, O Come, O Come Immanuel, and others."*

CHAPTER 2

The First Colleges in America Were Christian Colleges

Rev. John Harvard

Christians also built the first colleges and Universities in America. Christians built Harvard in 1638, Yale in 1701, Princeton in 1746, and Dartmouth in 1754.

The Original Mission

The original mission of these colleges was to train men for the ministry. Harvard was established when Rev. John Harvard donated his personal library and $5,000.00 to start the school.

In the 17th century, 52% of the men who graduated from Harvard entered the ministry. In 1646, Harvard adopted *Rules & Precepts*. Read this carefully and compare this to what is being taught at Harvard today.

"Everyone shall consider that the main end of his life and studies is to know God and Jesus Christ which is eternal life." (The Rebirth of America, Philadelphia: Arthur DeMoss Foundation, 1986, page 41)

The University of Florida

The University of Florida began as The East Florida Seminary in 1853 and became the first state-sponsored institution of higher learning in the State of Florida. All of the professors were Christians and all of the students attended church regularly on Sunday.

CHAPTER 3

Many Leading Scientists Were Christians

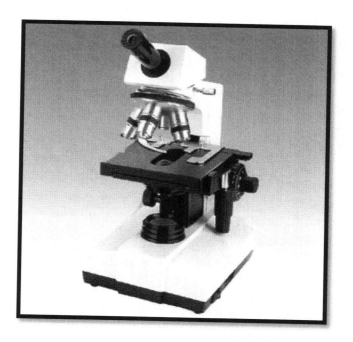

Christians not only built most of the first schools and colleges in America, in addition to that, many of the great scientists and inventors in history were Bible-believing Christians. Consider the following list of scientists which appeared in The Biblical Basis for Modern Science by the late Dr. Henry Morris, pages 463-464.

DISCIPLINE	SCIENTIST
Antiseptic Surgery	Joseph Lister
Bacteriology	Louis Pasteur
Calculus	Isaac Newton
Celestial Mathematics	Johann Kepler
Chemistry	Robert Boyle
Comparative Anatomy	Georges Cuvier
Computer Science	Charles Babbage
Dimensional Analysis	Lord Rayleigh
Dynamics	Isaac Newton
Electrodynamics	James Clark Maxwell
Electromagnetic	Michael Faraday
Electronics	Ambrose Fleming
Energetic	Lord Kelvin
Entom. of living insects	Henri Fabre
Field Theory	Michael Faraday

Fluid Mechanics	George Stokes
Gas dynamics	Robert Boyle
Genetics	Gregory Mendel
Glacial Geology	Louis Agassiz
Gynaecology	James Simpson
Hydraulics	Leonardo ad Vinci
Hydrograph	Matthew Mary
Hydrostatics	Blasé Pascal
Ichthyology	Louis Agassiz
Isotopic Chemistry	William Ramsey
Model Analysis	Lord Rayleigh
Natural History	John Ray
Non-Euclidean Geometry	Bernhard Riemann
Oceanography	Matthew Mary
Optical Mineralogy	David Brewster
Palaeontology	John Woodard
Pathology	Rudolph Virchow
Physical Astronomy	Johann Kepler

Reversible Thermodynamics	James Joule
Statistical Thermodynamics	James Clark Maxwell
Stratigraphy	Nicholas Steno
Systematic Biology	Carolos Linnaeus
Thermodynamics	Lord Kelvin
Thermo kinetics	Humphrey Davy
Vertebrate Palaeontology	Georges Cuvier
Absolute Temperature scale	Lord Kelvin
Actuarial Table	Charles Babbage
Barometer	Blasé Pascal
Biogenesis Law	Louis Pasteur
Calculating Machine	Charles Babbage
Chloroform	James Simpson
Classification System	Carolos Linnaeus
Double Stars	William Herschel
Electric Generator	Michael Faraday
Electric Motor	Joseph Henry
Ephemeris Table	Johann Kepler

Fermentation control	Louis Pasteur
Galvanometer	Joseph Henry
Global Star catalogue	John Herschel
Inert Gases	William Ramsey
Kaleidoscope	David Brewster
Law of Gravity	Isaac Newton
Mine Safety Lamp	Humphrey Davy
Pasteurization	Louis Pasteur
Reflecting telescope	Isaac Newton
Scientific Method	Francis Bacon
Self-induction	Joseph Henry
Telegraph	Samuel B. Morse
5 Thermionic Valve	Ambrose Fleming
Trans-Atlantic cable	Lord Kelvin
Vaccination and Immunization	Louis Pasteur
Electrodynamics	James Clerk Maxwell
Galactic Astronomy	William Herschel

CHAPTER 4

The Public School was Imported from Prussia

The school system which we commonly call the "public school" was imported from Prussia in the 1800's by politicians Horace Mann and Edward Everett. Both men were devout Humanists, and Governor Edward Everett of New York was a Unitarian pastor.

This Prussian School model was first introduced into the schools of Massachusetts and from there it spread to other states. Today, this Prussian, government controlled, secular, anti-Christian education model has totally replaced the original American Christian School system.

The Purpose of Public Schools

We want to stress again that both Horace Mann and Pastor Everett were devout Humanists and their objective was to move the schools out of the churches and get them under the ownership and control of the government like the schools they had seen in Prussia. If there is any doubt in your mind about this, please consider the remarks of Chester Pierce, Professor of Educational Psychiatry at

Harvard University, given at a Childhood Education Seminar in 1973.

"Every child in America entering school at the age of five is mentally ill, because he comes to school with certain allegiances toward our founding fathers, toward our elected officials, toward his parents, toward a belief in a supernatural Being, toward the sovereignty of this nation as a separate entity. It's up to you teachers to make all of these sick children well by creating the International child of the future."

Humanism Versus Christianity

"The battle for mankind's future must be waged and won in the public school classroom by teachers who correctly perceive their role as the proselytizers of a new faith. The classroom must and will become an arena of conflict between the old and the new. . . .the rotting corpse of Christianity and the new faith of Humanism." (Humanist, page 26 of the January/February 1983 issue).

Summary

The concept of a public schools neither an American or a Christian concept. What we call "public schools" are government schools controlled by teachers' unions and politicians.

CHAPTER 5

The Difference Between Public Schools and Christian Schools

How many people do you know who could write an intelligent paragraph explaining the difference between a public school and a Christian school?

The Question

What if we placed a Christian principal in every public school; placed a Christian teacher in every public school classroom; placed a Bible on every desk; and began every day with prayer. Would that school be a Christian school?

The Answer

No! That school would not be a Christian school. Adding Christians, Bibles, and prayers would not make that school a Christian school. One word makes the difference between a Christian school and a public school. Do you know what that one word is? That one word is philosophy.

Philosophy

The real difference between public (government) schools and Christian schools is one word and that one word is philosophy. The philosophy of every Christian school is Biblical Theism. The philosophy of every government school is secular humanism.

Secular Humanism

Humanism is the philosophy of every public school in America. There are no exceptions. Sadly, there are very few pastors today, and fewer parents who seem to understand this or can even define humanism. This is tragic. It is imperative for parents who profess to be Christians to understand what humanism is, especially when 90% of their children attend public schools and are being indoctrinated in humanism every day.

FIVE DOCTRINES OF SECULAR HUMANISM

1. Atheism

The philosophy of every public school in America is humanism and humanism denies the existence of God. Humanists are atheists. No Christian principal can change this. No Christian teacher can change this. No Christian school board can change this. There have even been lawsuits filed because students dared to mention the name of God, Jesus Christ, or the Bible in their valedictorian addresses.

2. The Theory of Evolution

Since humanists reject a belief in God, they must next explain man's existence independent of God. For this they resurrect one of the oldest religious beliefs of all time: the theory of evolution, which can be traced back to Babylon 2000 years before Christ."

Students who fail to go along with the theory of evolution face unbelievable discrimination from teachers. In Iowa, one professor stated that *he believed he should be allowed to fail any student he discovers believing in creation.* The professor desires to fail the student regardless of his/her grade point average. Another professor suggested that they be allowed to take back student's grades if the professor learns that the student embraces creation even after graduation. *So much for academic freedom.*

3. No Moral Absolutes

Christians believe that morals are absolute. Certain things are right and certain things are wrong. Humanists reject this.

Humanists teach our children that all morals are relative. The only thing a humanist is absolutely sure of is, that there are no absolutes.

Humanists encourage fornication and pass out condoms.

Humanists tell students that same sex marriage is acceptable and bully those who believe it is wrong.

Humanists tell students that adultery is permissible. In fact, in some schools, parents must sign a paper to prevent the school from giving condoms and birth control pills to their children.

There are no moral absolutes in any public school in America.

4. The Deification of Man

Humanists believe man is supreme. Man is the highest authority. Man makes the final decisions in everything. The final authority in all matters is the section of flesh between man's two ears. *Man is god!*

5. The Socialist One World View

Humanists believe in the innate goodness of man to govern the world equitably. Humanists love the United Nations. In the July/August 1966 issue of the Humanist magazine, the author admitted humanism's purpose was: *"To supersede nationalistic boundaries by a worldwide organization that would possess international sovereignty over the nations of the world."*

Humanism is also a Religion

According to the U.S. Supreme Court, humanism is a religion. (*Tornado v Watkins. 1961*). There is no such thing as a "neutral" school. The truth is, humanism is both a philosophy and a religion.

When humanists want to qualify for 501 C 3 tax exempt status, they hide behind a facade of religion.

When humanists want to maintain control of America's school system, or file lawsuits against religion in the schools, they quickly run and hide behind their "secular" position. According to the U.S. Supreme Court, humanism is a religion.

Religion is Taught in Every Public School

The truth is, religion is taught in every public school in America. Here are examples of humanism that is taught in our public-school classrooms. Here are some specific examples.

God

"God is different for different people, and there are many gods - - Allah, Shiva, Jesus, or no god at all. One should not judge all are equally acceptable. One should not judge another person's view of god."

Truth

"Truth changes with time, culture, situations, and individuals. If I believe something sincerely, it is true for me."

Morality

"Morality cannot be legislated. No one should compel his moral code upon others."

Marriage

"Marriage is dissolvable if it doesn't work out. A family is two or more people who love each other. Homosexuals should be allowed to marry and have the same benefits as heterosexuals."

Sex

"Sex is for consenting persons. Homosexuality is an alternate, acceptable lifestyle, which should be accepted as normal."

Abortion

"Abortion is a matter of personal choice."

Money

"Money is worthy of your life's pursuits, providing meaning and purpose. A person with many possessions will be happy."

The Universe

"The universe, nature, and humanity are the result of natural processes and random chance. God does not need to enter the picture."

The Bible

"The Bible is a book like many others, with no legitimate claim to truth over other books." (Southern Baptist Association of Christian Schools. www.sbacs.org (407) 808-9100)

Philosophy Makes the Difference

The real difference between a Christian school and a government (public) school is one word and that one word is "philosophy!"

FIVE DOCTRINES OF BIBLICAL THEISM

The philosophy of a truly Christian school is Biblical Theism. Humanism is the wisdom of man. Biblical Theism is the wisdom of God. Biblical Theism is also based on five doctrines.

1. Belief in God.

2. Special Creation and Intelligent Design.

3. Moral Absolutes. Some things are Right and some things are Wrong.

4. Man is a child of God, a servant and a steward of God. Man's Purpose on earth is to Glorify God.

5. Individualism, Nationalism, and the Rejection of the One-world government and the concept of a One-world court.

The real difference between a Christian school and a government (public) school is one word and that one word is "philosophy!"

The philosophy of a truly Christian school is Biblical Theism. The philosophy of every public school is humanism. Biblical Theism is the wisdom of God. Humanism is the wisdom of man. There are no exceptions.

Summary

1. What one word describes the real difference between a Christian school and a public school?

2. Can you name the five doctrines of secular humanism that are taught in every public school in America?

3. What is the philosophy of a truly Christian school?

4. Can you explain the five doctrines of Biblical Theism?

CHAPTER 6

The Battle for the Schools is Over and Christians Lost!

For years, public schools had reflected the values and standards of the community, and rightly so. Parents had confidence in their elected officials. Parents trusted their teachers. Many of those teachers who taught Sunday school on Sunday also taught in public school on Monday. Parents felt that it was safe for them to send their sons and daughters to public schools. They even prayed and read the Bible regularly. Parents believed that their children would actually receive a good education there. Parents believed that their schools reflected the values of their community and that it was the job of the school to reinforce these values and pass these values on to their children.

Those Days are History

Today's schools reflect the values of the government, not those of the parents. In many cases, the schools deliberately turn the children against their parents. Today, there is a concerted effort to replace the parent's values with those of the "change agents."

Christians Can't Change Public Schools

An interesting thing happened in Lake County, Florida, back in 1994. Some conservative Christians were elected to the school board and they tried to make reforms by adopting a new policy simply instructing teachers in Lake County to teach that **"the American culture is superior to others."**

School Superintendents' Response

School Superintendent, Tom Sanders, expressed publicly that he didn't know what the school board was talking about. He said: *"I'm having trouble getting people to tell me what the American Culture is, and what culture are we talking about?"*

Teachers Unions' Response

It was not surprising to see the local teachers' union, led by Gail Burry, to file a lawsuit contending that *"the new policy breaks Florida Law that requires schools to teach multiculturalism."*

This was not surprising because teachers' unions consistently oppose all attempts to reform the failed public schools.

Multiculturalism was Required by Florida Law

Back in 1994 I wondered why the schools couldn't teach that our American culture was superior to others. I now understand why our schools can't even teach that our American culture is even good, much less superior. I understood only after I did some research on multiculturalism.

An Attack on Western Culture

The Teacher's Union of Lake County was right. State law did require that public schools in all districts teach multiculturalism. (*Citrus Chronicle, Thursday, May 12, 1994, page 4a*)

I discovered that multiculturalism involves much more than the appreciation of other cultures.

- *Students in public schools today are being taught that the injustices of Western culture so far outweigh its virtues, that we should not even mention its virtues.*

- *Students in public schools are being taught that Western culture is degrading.*

- Students are being taught that euro-centric, western, American, culture is to blame for most of the evils that exist in the world today.

- Students in public schools are being taught to bash "dominant, white, males."

How Did it Happen?

How did humanism gain so much control over America? Consider what popular Christian author Tim LaHaye wrote:

"During the past 200 years, humanism (man's wisdom) has captivated the thinking of the Western world.

After conquering Europe's colleges and universities, it spread to America, where it developed a stranglehold on all public education.

Recognizing as they did the strategic nature of both education and the communications field in waging their battle for the minds of mankind, the humanist gradually moved in, until they virtually controlled both.

Almost every major magazine, newspaper, TV network, secular book publisher, and movie producer is a committed humanist, (our emphasis) surrounding himself with editors and newscasters who share his philosophy and seldom permit anything to be presented that contradicts humanism, unless enforced to by community pressure."

What have been the results of years of the humanistic indoctrination of our nations' students? Humanism has produced some bitter fruit in this nation.

Dr. D. James Kennedy

Consider the remarks of the late Dr. D. James Kennedy as he addressed the subtle takeover of humanism in America.

"There has been no outcry, no public indignation, no articles in Time or Newsweek critiquing this new religion. No talk show has dissected it to discover its roots and resolves.

Indeed, almost silently has the newest religion in America taken over a large segment of our national population, and most of those who have 'joined' don't even know they have been indoctrinated.

This religion now has more houses of worship, more preachers, more property, more audiences, more power, more money, and more control than any other religion in America.

So subtle has been its takeover of the substructure of the American way of life that most people don't even know its name. It is the religion of Secular Humanism."

The Battle for the Schools is Over and Christians Lost!

Well-meaning pastors and church members who are still dreaming of reforming public schools remind me of those poor Japanese soldiers who were found living in caves in the Pacific many years after the war had ended. Nobody had told them the war was over and that Japan had lost. Our church pews are filled with people like that. It's time to wake up! That war was over long ago. Christians lost! Humanists won!!

Summary

1. Why does the author believe the battle for the schools is over and Christians lost?

2. Do you believe Christians working in public schools can change public schools? Give examples.

CHAPTER 7

The Deplorable State of Education Today

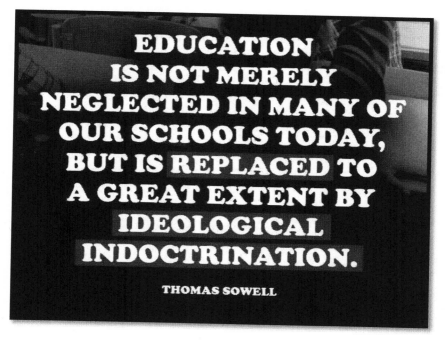

EDUCATION IS NOT MERELY NEGLECTED IN MANY OF OUR SCHOOLS TODAY, BUT IS REPLACED TO A GREAT EXTENT BY IDEOLOGICAL INDOCTRINATION.

THOMAS SOWELL

In our opinion, humanism has virtually destroyed American education. Humanism is now the official philosophy (and religion) in every public school and state college in America.

America is in Deep Trouble

We spend more money on education than any other industrialized nation, but our children have the poorest education. When our children are tested, we score near the bottom of all industrialized nations.

The Most Illiterate Period in History

There was a time when Americans were the best educated people in the world. This is no longer true. Did you realize that the American farmers of the eighteenth and nineteenth centuries were better educated than some of our college graduates of today? We now are living in the most illiterate period in American history. According to a study conducted in late April 2018 by the US Department of Education and the National Institute of literacy:

- 32 million adults in the United States can't read. That's 14 percent of the population.

- 21 percent of the adults in the U.S. read below the 5th grade level.

- 19 percent of high school graduates can't read.

The Role of Public School Teachers

What is the role of a teacher in the public school today? Here is the view of Chester Pierce, Professor of Educational Psychiatry at Harvard University, given at a Childhood Education Seminar in 1973.

"Every child in America entering school at the age of five is mentally ill, because he comes to school with certain allegiances

toward our founding fathers, toward our elected officials, toward his parents, toward a belief in a supernatural Being, toward the sovereignty of this nation as a separate entity. It's up to you teachers to make all of these sick children well by creating the International child of the future." **(http://quotes.liberty-tree.ca/quote_blog/Chester.Pierce.Quote.FF38***)*

Public School Textbooks

In an article titled, *"Textbooks on Trial,"(Wheaton: 1976, page 14)* James C. Hefley exposed some of the ideas that are found in public school textbooks today. Here is one example:

"Allegiance to a nation is the biggest stumbling block to the creation of International government. National boundaries and the concept of sovereignty must be abolished. The quickest way to abolish sovereignty is to condition the young people to another and broader allegiance. Opinion favourable to international government will be developed in the social studies in the elementary schools."

A Cultural War

Pat Buchannan has been criticized for talking about a *"cultural war."* The fact is, every knowledgeable educator knows that there's been a cultural war raging for years. *The Humanist,* an organ of the American Humanist Association addressed this "cultural war" on *page 26 of the January/February 1983 issue.* Here is what the article said:

"The battle for mankind's future must be waged and won in the public-school classroom by teachers who correctly perceive their role as the proselytizers of a new faith. The classroom must

and will become an arena of conflict between the old and the new. . . .the rotting corpse of Christianity and the new faith of Humanism."

What educator doesn't know that the arena for this conflict is the classroom of the public school?

Multiculturalism in Disguise

Multiculturalism was introduced into our schools disguised as a way "to make Americans more sensitive to the diverse cultural back-grounds of the people of this country."This sounds good, but this is not what multiculturalism is all about. To understand multiculturalism, it is necessary to define certain "buzz" words that are associated with it.

Abraham Lincoln

Abraham Lincoln once said, *"You can't make the short man taller by cutting off the giants' legs."* You don't teach students to be more sensitive to the diverse cultural backgrounds of other people by depriving them of a decent education. Multiculturalism deprives students of a decent education and teaches them lies instead, just to make them feel good about themselves.

Tolerance

The first word is "tolerance." I've yet to meet a parent who can even define this word. We "think" we can, but the word "tolerance" today doesn't mean what it did when we went to school. Most of us would define tolerance as "putting up with something." That's not what it means today. That's not what it means to your sons and daughters either.

Today's Definition of Tolerance

"All ideas, all lifestyles, all values, are equal. No idea, or value, is superior to another. Anyone who differs with this concept is called intolerant."

This is why it is not possible to teach that American culture is superior. The very thought of this is degrading. *"How do you think that makes other cultures feel?"* asks the multiculturalists.

This is why we hear less and less about justice in school today. The concept of "justice" requires a set of standards and a value system where some things are right, and some things are wrong. *"A tolerant" person accepts all ideas, beliefs, lifestyles, as being equal. Therefore, there can be no "right or wrong." All are equal.*

No Moral Absolutes

A Christian, for example, who believes in absolute moral values, is labelled as "intolerant," and most students fear being labelled "intolerant."

Pluralistic Society

Back in the sixties and seventies, we heard a lot about America being a "pluralistic" society. What is a pluralistic society? A pluralistic society is a society that is in transition. It is a society that is exchanging one set of values for another. The United States went through a transition period in which our philosophy changed from "Biblical Theism," to "Secular Humanism."

The Melting Pot is Out. The Salad Bar is In

The Multiculturalists hate the idea of America being called a "melting pot." That suggests assimilation. The new concept is that America is a "salad bar." Multiculturalism is essentially an attack on Western civilization. Multiculturalism is an attack on America's traditional system of values. Multiculturalism is an attack on Christianity itself.

Rev. Jesse Jackson

This war on Western culture is not new. A few years ago, the Rev. Jesse Jackson led a demonstration at Stanford University. The protestors marched across the campus *chanting "Hey, Hey, Ho, Ho, Western Culture's Got to Go."* The administration gave in to these demands and scrapped the Western civilization requirement.

Yale University

A few years ago, a Texas billionaire gave Yale University $20 million to establish a Chair of Western Civilization. The administration established a Chair of Multiculturalism instead. Angry students wrote the alumni who wrote the donor. The donor reminded the university that the money had been given to establish a chair of Western Civilization. The university informed the donor that "There would be no Chair of Western Civilization on Yale's campus." The donor promptly forced the university to return the money.

Western History

It is tragic today that a student can graduate from college and never take one course or read one book on Western History, which, by the way, is our heritage. A late 1980's survey by the Association of American Colleges ascertained that a student could graduate from 78% of our colleges and universities without taking one Western History course.

Literature

One could graduate from 45% of the colleges and universities without taking one literature course. Yet, a student today *cannot even attend* a college or university without getting a dose of multiculturalism.

Blame America First

Multiculturalism does not allow us to teach that the American Culture is superior. We can't even teach that the American culture is good. Multiculturalists teach our children that America's injustices so far outweigh her virtues that we shouldn't even mention America's virtues.

- Do you agree that schools should teach students that Western Culture is degrading?

- Do you agree that students should be taught to bash white males?

- Do you believe that schools should teach your child that Columbus discovered America, or that Columbus invaded America?

- Do you want the best history and literature books banned and censored just because they happen to have been written by Western authors or dead, white, European males?

- Do you agree that history should be revised, and facts eliminated, and myths be taught to your child, just so minority students will "feel good" about themselves?

- Did you know that students today are being taught that Africans really discovered America by crossing the Atlantic on rafts, hundreds of years before Columbus?

- Did you know that students are taught that the ideas found in the U.S. Constitution were really borrowed from the Iroquois Indians?

- Did you know that students are taught that the ancient Greeks and Romans stole all their ideas from the Egyptians who were black?

- Did you know that just about everything wrong in the world today can be blamed on Columbus and dominant, Euro-American, White Males?

Great Books Banned

Do you really want your sons and daughters to graduate from college without even being exposed to the great works of the past? The works of Aristotle, Locke, and Shakespeare, are censored, and in their place, students are forced-fed the writings of third-rate feminist and minority writers who attack Western civilization as sexist, racist, and oppressive. (*Phyllis Schlafley Report, "Colleges Should Display Warning Labels". April 1994, p. 1*).

Did you know that students can graduate from college today without even being exposed to any of the great works of any U.S. or British authors like Melville, Hawthorne, Poe, Dickenson, Whitman,

Faulkner, Donne, Bacon, Coleridge, Wordsworth, Browning, Tennyson, or Dickens? These great books of Western culture are banned because they were written by "dead, white, European, males."

Ivy League professor, Jeffrey Hart, reminds us: *"You can graduate from Dartmouth without ever having been required to study a play by Shakespeare."* Students are, however required to take one course in "non-western culture.""This requirement," said Hart, *"can be satisfied by going for one term to St. Petersburg, Florida."(Jeffrey Hart, "A good college education is still possible." King Features Syndicate, Inc.)*

Teachers Are Now Facilitators

There's a reason you cannot get a good education in a public school. Very few teachers' colleges even believe teachers should impart knowledge. They view themselves as facilitators instead of teachers.

Survey of High School Students

Consider the results of one survey of some American high school students of today.

- 34 % of the public-school students surveyed knew the island in "Survivor" is in the South Pacific, but only 30 % of them could find the state of New Jersey on a map of the United States.

- 50 % of the students could not find New York on a map of the United States.

- 30 % of the students couldn't even find the Pacific Ocean on a map of the world.

- Only 13 % of the students surveyed could find Iraq on a map of the world.

Santa Fe College in Gainesville, Florida

An English Literature professor at Santa Fe Community College wrote an essay about his students that attracted nationwide attention. He wrote:

- "They know little history. . .

- I have received as answers to test questions that: George Washington's cherry tree was biblical. . .

- Pearl Harbour was in Vietnam . . .

- The video camera was the device that provided a visual chronicle of the Civil War."

- Few of them read during the downtime between classes, preferring to sit and stare at others or reapply their cosmetics.

- The professor said that his students' writing is worse. He said: "My students are shocked to be expected to read or produce more than a sound bite."

- "Hundreds of them have claimed to be unable to generate three pages on any subject."

- "They rely on pictographs, like cavemen." (The Gainesville Sun, Wednesday, February 12, 2003. Page 10A).

Immorality Today

The number of unmarried teens getting pregnant has nearly doubled in the last 20 years. We believe this is directly related to the rejection of all moral values in our schools. Teenage promiscuity has reached the point where:

- *60,069,971 babies have been murdered by abortion Since Roe v Wade in 1973.*

- *2,899 children are murdered by abortion every day.*

- *120 children are murdered by abortion every hour.*

- *One child is murdered by abortion every second.*

- *Some Schools are not even allowed to teach abstinence.*

Illegal to Teach Abstinence

According to Mona Carranza, a judge in Shreveport, La. has ruled that *teaching abstinence may not be a part of a sex education program for high school students.* *"Abstinence,* "said the judge (urged on by Planned Parenthood, who filed suit), *"is a religiously based virtue. To teach it in public schools is to violate the separation of church and state."*

Illegal to Display the 10 Commandments

Now before you laugh, consider this: It has long been illegal to display the Ten Commandments in public classrooms, and the Supreme Court recently held that a milquetoast, ecumenical, watered-down invocation of God's blessing on graduating high school seniors was also a violation of the Constitution.

None Dare Call It Education

We recommend any serious pastors and parents who may read this to secure a copy of the book, *None Dare Call it Education*, by John Stormer. Here are just a few examples of what the author reveals about today's public-school textbooks.

- There are direct quotes from public school text books instructing children ages 5-8 on sexual intercourse.

- Pages 171-196 provide details of sex education that children are being exposed to as early as kindergarten.

- There are instructions for grades 6-12 on having oral sex.

Condoms on Cucumbers

Another powerful book is Michael Savage's book, "The Enemy Within," which was on the New York Best Seller list. *Chapter 8 is Titled, SCHOOLS: Condoms on Cucumbers.* Read about games teachers are instructed to play with their students. Read it and weep.

Candy Canes Banned

ELKHORN, Nebraska — The Rutherford Institute has offered to assist the Elkhorn Public Schools should they encounter any fallout as a result of their decision to overturn Principal Jennifer Sinclair's attempt to purge Manchester Elementary School of any symbol or mention of Christmas, *including singing Christmas carols, using items that have red/green colors, and candy canes which were perceived as problematic because the shape is a 'J' for Jesus.*

- Teachers at a Connecticut school were instructed to change the wording of "Twas the Night Before Christmas" to "Twas the Night Before a Holiday."

- A high school principal in Virginia was unsure about whether he could mention Santa or distribute candy canes after a Muslim family objected to them as symbols of Christmas.

- A public-school principal in Minnesota won't even allow "Season's Greetings" to be used in school publications.

Manger Scenes Banned

Things are not much better outside the schools: In one West Virginia town, although the manger scene (one of 350 light exhibits in the town's annual Festival of Lights) included shepherds, camels and a guiding star. The main attractions (Jesus, Mary and Joseph) were nowhere to be found. *(https://freedomoutpost.com/school-principal-prohibits-christmas-symbols-words-colors-red-and-green-candy-canes-carols/)*

Anti-Christian Era

We have seen America evolve from a *Christian era*, through a *Post-Christian era*, and finally to an *Anti-Christian era*. Each year, there are new attacks on God, Christ, and religious symbols. In one school in North Carolina, a little girl got into trouble for reading a letter her grandfather had written from the battlefield in World War II. *The letter mentioned that the men called on God for help.*

I served in the ministry for more than half a century, serving as the pastor of the same church in a university community (Gainesville, Florida) since 1959. I have also been involved in

Christian education for more than forty years, and I am convinced that the real problem is the godless, secular, humanistic, government schools where those students have spent the past twelve years of their lives. When students graduate from public schools, they may still be members of our churches, but actually, they are "certified" Humanists. It's like saying their hearts are saved but their heads are lost!

Definition of Insanity

Someone said that the definition of insanity is "doing the same thing over and over and expecting a different result."

The philosophy of a truly Christian School is Biblical Theism. The philosophy of every public school in America is humanism. No teacher can change this. No principal can change this. No school board can change this. There are no exceptions.

Parents who want their children to be indoctrinated in secular humanism should send them to public schools.

Parents who want their children to be taught Biblical Theism must send them to Christian schools or teach them at home.

There are no other options!

CHAPTER 8

Why 80% of the Youth Leave Our Churches and Never Return

It is past time for pastors and church members to wake up to the fact, that even if our children do spend an hour or two in church on Sundays, it is not going to make much difference, or even come close to solving the problem. It's time to face the cold hard facts of life.

We urge every pastor and Christian parent to read the book **Already Gone** by Ken Ham & Britt Beemer. It is available at Amazon.com. This book documents the fact that more than 80 % of the young people in our churches who attend public schools, will leave those churches when they graduate from high school and never return. The truth is, their minds have already left church while they were in middle school. The only reason they are still in church is because they are still living at home.

The Deplorable State of the Post- Modern Church

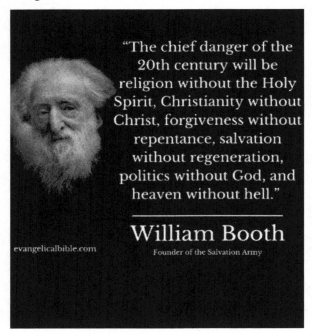

"The chief danger of the 20th century will be religion without the Holy Spirit, Christianity without Christ, forgiveness without repentance, salvation without regeneration, politics without God, and heaven without hell."

William Booth

Founder of the Salvation Army

evangelicalbible.com

25% of Today's Pastors Are Atheists

You may find this hard to believe but there are many churches today who have pastors who don't even believe in God. Yet, they stand in their pulpits every Sunday and put on a show. If you doubt this, go on Google and type in "What percentage of pastors are atheist?" and look at all of the information on this subject.

Many Pastors Are Not Even Christians

In one survey of 7,441 Protestant pastors, the following numbers did not even believe in the physical resurrection of Jesus from the dead. This means they are not even Christians, yet they stand in their pulpits and mislead people every Sunday.

- 51 % of the Methodists,

- 35 % of the Presbyterians,

- 30 % of the Episcopalians,

- 33 % of the American Baptists

Many Pastors Reject the Bible

In another survey, 7,441 Protestant pastors were asked if they believed that the Bible is the inspired, inerrant Word of God. (Pulpit Helps, December 1987)

- 95% of Episcopalians said no!

- 87% of Methodists said no!

- 82% of Presbyterians said no!

- 67% of American Baptists said no!.

Only 51% Have a Biblical World View

George Barna reported that only half of the country's Protestant pastors (51%) have a Biblical worldview. Have you ever wondered why so few pastors today even have a Biblical world view? In our opinion, it is because most of those pastors probably graduated from public schools and attended state colleges where they were indoctrinated with secular humanism.

What is a Biblical World View?

A Biblical world view is believing that absolute moral truth exists, that it is based upon the Bible, and having a biblical view on six core beliefs. Those six core beliefs are:

1. The accuracy of Biblical teaching,

2. The sinless nature of Jesus.

3. The literal existence of Satan.

4. The Omnipotence and Omniscience of God.

5. Salvation is by Grace alone.

6. The personal responsibility to evangelize.

The researcher produced data showing that there are significant variations by denominational affiliation and other demographics. The Southern Baptists had the highest percentage of pastors with a biblical worldview (71%) while the Methodists were lowest among the seven segments evaluated (27%).

Many pastors fail to   with the issues that will protect their young people from the indoctrination they receive in public school every week on subjects like the LGBT movement and abortion. Those pastors tickle people's ears and tell them what they want to hear to make them feel good. All they seem to care about is nickels and noses.

Same-sex married couple to lead historic Baptist church

NEWS BOB ALLEN | JANUARY 9, 2017

3.2K

A historic Baptist church in the nation's capital has called a legally married lesbian couple as co-pastors.

Calvary Baptist Church in Washington announced Jan. 9

Biblical Ignorance in the Church Today

The Bible warned us that in the last days, churches will depart from the faith. That is happening in many churches today.

"Now the Spirit speaketh expressly, that in the latter times some shall depart from the faith, giving heed to seducing spirits, and doctrines of devils." (I Timothy 4:1)

R. Albert Jr. wrote an interesting article on Biblical illiteracy in the Church. He wrote: **"Americans revere the Bible, but, by and large, they don't read it. And because they don't read it, they have become a nation of biblical illiterates."**

- Fewer than half of all adults can name the four gospels.

- Many Christians cannot identify more than two or three of the disciples.

- 60 percent of Americans can't name even five of the Ten Commandments.

- 12 percent of adults believe that Joan of Arc was Noah's wife.

- Another survey of graduating high school seniors revealed that over 50 percent thought that Sodom and Gomorrah were husband and wife.

- A considerable number of respondents to one poll indicated that the Sermon on the Mount was preached by Billy Graham.

Summary

Is there any question as to why more than 80% of our young people will leave church following graduation and never return? Students spend a maximum of 156 hours a year in church (if they are never absent). 3 hours x 52 weeks = 156 hours per year in church. They spend 156 hours per year x 12 years = 1,872 hours in church by the time they graduate from high school. .

During that same time, they spend 7 hours per day for 5 days every week in public school. This is to total of 35 hours every week. They spend 180 days every year in public school. This means 7 hours per day for 180 days = 1,260 hours per year being indoctrinated in humanism. They spend 12 years (not including kindergarten) before graduation.

This is 1,260 hours x 12 years = 15,120 hours by the time they graduate, where it is illegal to hear from the Bible, but where they are being indoctrinated in humanism.

I am convinced that if Christians are going to obey God's Word and train their children according to His Word it can't possibly be done in 2 hours on Sunday Morning and perhaps an hour on Wednesday night.

There are only two solutions for Christian parents who want their children to receive a real education. Enrol them in a Christian school or teach them at home

CHAPTER 9

Sixty Reasons Why Christian Parents Should Send Their Children To Christian Schools

Does it really matter where your children attend school? In the opinion of this present writer, this is one of the most important decisions you will ever make. If you are a Christian, your child should attend a Christian school. May we give you sixty reasons why?

1. Christian Schools are the True <u>American Schools</u>.

2. Christian Schools meet in the <u>Right Place</u>.

Christian schools, like the first American schools, are held in the right place, and the right place is the local church, not the local government building.

3. Christian Schools have the <u>Right Philosophy</u>.

The philosophy of a true Christian school is *Biblical Theism* (like the first American schools). Students in a Christian school are trained to view all of life from God's point of view. *Humanism* is the official philosophy of every government school in America. There are no exceptions.

4. Christian Schools have the <u>Right Teachers</u>.

All of the teachers in Christian schools are born-again, educated, trained, dedicated members of the local Bible preaching church. There are no atheist, socialist, sodomites, lesbians, pantheist, or globalist teaching in our school. Christian school teachers believe their work is a ministry and not just a job. Christian school teachers are ministers, not change agents or facilitators.

5. Christian Schools have the <u>Right Curriculum</u>.

Christian schools, like the first American schools, use textbooks that are based on the Bible. They teach the truth about God, creation, history, morals, and Western Culture. We believe that wisdom, knowledge and understanding come from God and it is not possible for a child to receive a true education when God and the Bible are not allowed. As we mentioned earlier, Noah Webster was a born-again Christian and he considered education useless without the Bible.

6. Christian Schools are <u>Controlled by Parents</u>, not Teachers Unions and Politicians.

In public schools, the parents provide all of the students and all of the money, yet they have no control or any "say so" over what is taught. The public schools are owned by the government and controlled by the teachers' unions. Politicians decide where your children go to school, how long they will stay, and what they will learn.

In Christian Schools, parents exercise choice. They can choose to send their children to a Christian school, teach them at home, or send them to public schools.

7. Christian Schools teach <u>children to Read</u> in Kindergarten and in the First Grade.

The first responsibility of any school system is to teach children to read. Christian schools teach children to read (the right way) in kindergarten and in the first grade. There are over one hundred scientific studies that prove the superiority of phonics over the "look-say" method of learning to read.

Students in Countryside Christian School and Riverside Christian School are divided into two groups: Students who are *learning to read*, and students who are *reading to learn*.

Students who are learning to read (kindergarten and first grade) are placed in a traditional type classroom where we use the ABEKA curriculum which is strong on phonics.

Kathy Smith Has Been Teaching Kids to Read for 30 Years

Students who are reading to learn (grades 2-12) are placed in a Learning Center where the learning is *individualized*, and students are not held back with the "pack," but are allowed to progress as far and as fast as they are capable of progressing. The learning is *accelerated*, the curriculum is totally *Christian*, and the result is a balanced, quality *education (ACE = Accelerated Christian Education)*.

8. Christian Schools are free to <u>Teach Students the Bible</u>.

The Bible is God's inspired Word. It is a lamp unto our feet and a light unto our paths. God's people should read it, believe it, memorize it, and obey it. Sadly, though, the church today is filled with Biblical illiterates.

Christian schools are as different as night and day. In our school (Countryside Christian in Gainesville, Florida) we have a different Scripture assigned every month.

In our school, students are exposed to the Bible every day. each month there is a different section of Scripture assigned. Students are encouraged and rewarded for memorizing their monthly Scriptures.

At the end of the school year, we have an awards night. The largest trophies are earned by students who can recite ALL monthly Scriptures at one time with no help.

Awards Night – Countryside Christian School

How many hours does the average young person who attends church, but who attends a public school, spend learning and memorizing the Bible? How much Scripture do you think the average child or teenager in a public school memorizes each year?

I would like to see how many Sunday school teachers in the Gainesville area could quote as much Scripture as one of our first graders in Countryside Christian School.

9. Christian Schools teach students the truth about <u>Charles Darwin</u> and the <u>Theory of Evolution</u>.

Charles Darwin was Not a Scientist.

Darwin dropped out of medical school after two years, changed majors, and earned a degree in Divinity. We call Darwin an apostate Divinity student. Yet, he is the author of the Origin of the Species, which is the Bible of the evolutionists.

Evolution is not happening today. It was never observed by anyone, at any time in the recorded history of man. It is a theory based on blind faith. It is widely accepted today because it is the only explanation students are allowed by law to hear.

What Difference Does It Make?

Why should Christians concern themselves with the theory of evolution or intelligent design? After all, if we believe God created everything, what difference does it make if He created the world instantly or used the process of evolution to develop everything gradually over long ages?

Ron Carlson said: "One of the most important questions that anyone can ask today is regarding the question of origins.

Today there are two competing philosophies on this issue. One is the theory of evolution, which says that men and women are merely an accident, evolved from slimy algae. The other view is Genesis 1:1, which says, "In the beginning God created."

How you answer the question of origins, whether you are an accident or a unique creation of God, will ultimately determine everything else in your life. This will determine your value for human individuals, your basis of morality, your meaning and purpose in life, and your ultimate destiny.

It is one of the most fundamental questions you can ask." (Carlson, Ron (2003-07-01). Fast Facts® on False Teachings (Kindle Locations 857-865). Harvest House Publishers. Kindle Edition.)

No One can have it Both Ways

The late Dr. D. James Kennedy reminded us that we cannot have it both ways. *"A naturalistic, evolutionary world view is more than a question of whether evolution has ever taken place on any scale, at any time, in any place. Rather it represents the complete antithesis of the Christian biblical world view. Either the Bible is true when it says a personal God created the heavens and earth and all it contains, or evolution is true. No one can have it both ways."*

We believe both true science and the Bible support intelligent design. We also want to look at the scientific evidence that points to the fact that you are not an accident, but a unique creation of an Almighty Loving Creator. There are more than 100 top scientists today who reject the popular theory of evolution that is taught in every public school in America.

10. Christian Schools teach students the truth about <u>Morality</u>. Some things are <u>Right and some things are Wrong</u>.

Can you find one public school text book in the State of Florida that teaches students the Ten Commandments and encourages students to obey them? We want to remind you again what is taught in every public school in America.

- *"Truth changes with time, culture, situations, and individuals. If I believe something sincerely, it is true for me."*

- *"Morality cannot be legislated. No one should compel his moral code upon others."*

- *"Marriage is dissolvable if it doesn't work out.*

- *A Family is two or more people who love each other.*

- *Homosexuals should be allowed to marry and have the same benefits as heterosexuals."*

- "Sex is for consenting persons.

- Homosexuality is an alternate, acceptable lifestyle, which should be accepted as normal."

- "Abortion is a matter of personal choice."

Christian schools teach the students the difference between right and wrong.

11. Christian Schools teach students the <u>Difference between Boys and Girls</u>.

When we are conceived in our mother's wombs, we are either male or female. This is a fact of science. In Christian Schools, boys and girls use separate restrooms, locker rooms, and showers. Teachers use accurate terms like "his and hers." This may sound old fashioned, but that's the way it is, and that's the way it should be.

12. Christian Schools teach students the <u>Difference between Socialism, Communism, & Capitalism</u>.

13. Christian School students learn the <u>Difference between True Science and "Junk Science</u>."

Consider the exhortation from Paul to Timothy in I Timothy 6:20:*"Timothy, keep that which is committed to thy trust, avoiding profane and vain babblings, and oppositions of <u>science falsely so called</u>."*

True Science is based on Observation and Experiment.

There's true Science and there is "junk" Science. True Science has always pointed to an intelligent Creator. Evolutionist can't tell us when, where, or how life began. Their theories require too much blind faith.

Spontaneous Generation, for example, is not scientific. It is accepted by blind faith. The fossil record reveals that life appeared suddenly and when it appeared it was already diversified and complex.

There are No Transitional Forms in the Fossil Record.

When confronted by the fact that there is no evidence of evolution in the fossil record, Charles Darwin gave the following feeble explanation: *"Geology assuredly does not reveal any such finely graded chain; and this is perhaps the most serious objection which can be urged against the theory. The explanation lies, however, in the extreme imperfection of the geologic record."Did you understand what Charles Darwin said? The explanation lies, however, in the extreme imperfection of the geologic record."*

Nothing x Chance x Time = Everything???

Where in the history of the world has anything come into existence without energy intelligently directed? Have you ever seen a master painting without a painter? Have you seen a large building or a bridge without an engineer? Look at the human eye. Look at the humming-bird. Look at DNA. Look at Laminin. What a marvellous, complex example of intelligent design.

Louis Pasteur

Louis Pasteur proved scientifically that life did not come from dead matter. This is a fact of true Science. Junk Science tells us that Nothing x Time x Chance = Everything. No reputable Scientist can point to even one scientifically observed and recorded instance of anything coming into existence out of a vacuum or coming into existence without energy intelligently directed. The reason is obvious!

14. Christian Schools Develop Character.

Students in public schools are taught that morals are relative and that there is nothing clearly right or wrong. Christian parents should want their children taught character traits and moral truths. Those truths include: Honesty, integrity, respect authority and individual rights. Students are taught to accept responsibility, to be fair, and to show compassion toward others. Students in a Christian school are taught that they have a responsibility to God, to their families, to their neighbours, and to their country.

The 60 Character traits of Jesus.

In ACE (Accelerated Christian Education) schools, the sixty character traits of Jesus Christ are woven into the curriculum. In government schools, you can't mention God or Jesus without the threat of a lawsuit.

The sports programs in Christian schools are also designed to build character, teamwork, respect for authority and physical discipline. I wonder how many young people in our churches who attend public schools could even name 10 of the 60 Character traits of Jesus. How about our Sunday school teachers?

15. Christian Schools teach students <u>When Life Begins</u> and the <u>Truth about Abortion</u>.

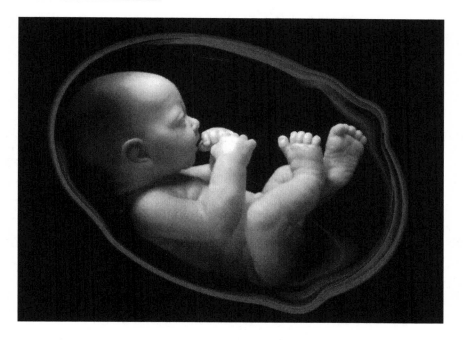

Biologically speaking, life begins at conception. The very moment the male sperm unites with the female egg, a brand- new life begins. Never in the past, or in the future, will there ever be another person like this one.

- The sex of the child is determined at conception.

- The color of the child's eyes is determined at conception.

- The color of the child's hair is determined at conception.

- The color of the child's skin is determined the moment the sperm is joined to the egg.

At the instant the male sperm meets the female egg, a unique human being (person) is created. The baby is not the mothers' body. The baby is being carried in the mothers' body. The fact that one of those bodies can die and the other body can live is proof that what we are talking about is two separate human beings. The pre-born child is a unique, separate, living, human being.

- At the instant the male sperm meets the female egg the little child has his or her own genetic code.

- By the tenth day after conception the little child's veins develop.

- By the fourteenth day after conception the little child's mouth begins to develop.

- By the 43rd day after the male sperm unites with the female egg, the child's brain-waves can be picked up on EEG.

- By the 56th day after conception, the tiny child's heart-beat can be recorded on EKG.

- In just 84 days (12 weeks) after the male sperm joins the female egg, (12 weeks), the little child is completely formed. In 84 days, all the organs the child will ever have are formed and functioning.

- In just <u>18 weeks</u> after conception the child could cry if there was any air in the womb.

- By this time the tiny child can swallow, suck his thumb, sleep, wake, and swim with a natural swimmer's stroke.

- Within just 84 days after the male sperm unites with the female egg the child is fully formed and nothing will be added except time, nutrition, and oxygen.

- Biologically, life begins at conception!

More children have been killed by abortion than lives lost in all of the wars in American history.

16. Christian Schools teach students that <u>God loves them</u> and has an exciting <u>plan for every life</u> (Jeremiah 29:11). *"For I know the plans I have for you, says the Lord. They are plans for good and not for disaster, to give you a future and a hope." (NLT).*

Students in public schools never hear this. Consider this quote from the book, Fast Facts on False Teaching, by Ron Carlson: (according to the Evolutionists).

- *"You are the descendant of a tiny cell of primordial protoplasm that washed up on an ocean beach 3½ billion years ago.*

- *You are the blind and arbitrary product of time, chance, and natural forces.*

- *Your closest living relatives swing from trees and eat crackers at the zoo.*

- *You are a mere grab bag of atomic particles, a conglomeration of genetic substance.*

- *You exist on a tiny planet in a minute solar system in an obscure galaxy in a remote and empty corner of a vast, cold, and meaningless universe.*

- *You are flying through lifeless space with no purpose, no direction, no control, and no destiny but final destruction.*

- *You are a purely biological entity, different only in degree but not in kind from a microbe, virus, or amoeba.*

- *You have no essence beyond your body, and at death you will cease to exist entirely.*

- *What little life you do have is confined to a fragile body aimlessly moving through a world plagued by war, famine, and disease.*

- The only question is whether the world will manage to blow itself up before your brief and pointless life ends on its own.

- In short, you came from nothing, you are going nowhere, and you will end your brief cosmic journey beneath six feet of dirt, where all that is you will become food for bacteria and rot with worms. (Carlson, Ron (2003-07-01). Fast Facts® on False Teachings (Kindle Locations 1067-1079). Harvest House Publishers. Kindle Edition.)

Students in Christian Schools learn that God loves them and has a definite plan for every life. They learn who Jesus is, why He came to earth, and that He will take them to heaven when they die if they repent of their sins and trust Him to be their Saviour. Students in public schools (and in many churches) today, never hear this.

17. Christian Schools teach students <u>How to Pray</u> and they pray in school every day.

18. Christian Schools teach students the truth about the <u>First Amendment</u> and expose the <u>Myth of Separation of Church and State</u>.

How Would You Like to Win $100.00Cash?

Find that phrase, *"Separation of Church and State,"* anywhere in our founding documents. Check the Declaration of Independence, the Constitution, and the Bill of Rights.

The **First Amendment** told the government that it <u>couldn't</u> pass any law that prohibited the free exercise of religion.

The **First Amendment** was designed to serve as a "one-way street" for the government.

The **First Amendment** was designed to keep the government's nose out of the church's business.

The **First Amendment** was designed to protect citizens from the government - - not to protect the government from the citizens.

In fact, the sole purpose of the Bill of Rights was to tell the <u>government what it could not do</u>, not to tell the church what it could not do.

Francis Schaeffer reminded us that the very Amendment that was designed to protect Christians from the government has been turned into a weapon to purge Christianity from this country. Writing in the "Christian Manifesto," he said:

"Today, the separation of church and state is used to silence the church...When Christians speak out on issues, the hue and cry from the humanist's state and media is that Christians, and all religions, are prohibited from speaking since there is a separation of church and state.

The way the concept is used today is totally reversed from its original intent. It is not rooted in history. The modern concept of separation is an argument for a total separation of religion from the state. The consequence of the acceptance of this doctrine leads to the removal of religion as an influence in civil government." (Schaeffer, p. 36)

19. Christian Schools teach students the <u>Truth about Love, Courtship and Marriage</u>.

Do you remember what is taught by the Humanist in government schools?

- "Marriage is dissolvable if it doesn't work out.

- A Family is two or more people who love each other.

- Homosexuals should be allowed to marry and have the same benefits as heterosexuals."

- "Sex is for consenting persons.

- Homosexuality is an alternate, acceptable lifestyle, which should be accepted as normal."

20. Christian Schools teach students the <u>Truth about Homosexuality</u> and <u>Same Sex </u>Relationships.

Would you like to know what the Bible says about this? We urge you to get a copy of our book on this subject. It is available from Amazon in Kindle and paperback.

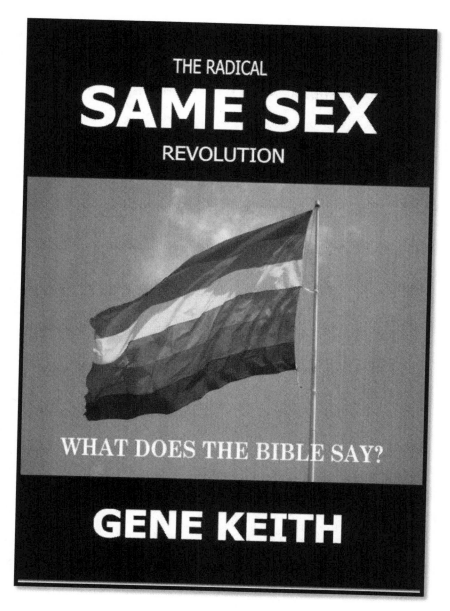

THE RADICAL

SAME SEX

REVOLUTION

WHAT DOES THE BIBLE SAY?

GENE KEITH

For a clear understanding about same sex relationships read the following Scriptures from the book of Romans

Romans 1:18-32

18 But God shows his anger from heaven against all sinful, evil men who push away the truth from them.

19 For the truth about God is known to them instinctively;[*] God has put this knowledge in their hearts.

20 Since earliest times men have seen the earth and sky and all God made, and have known of his existence and great eternal power. So they will have no excuse when they stand before God at Judgment Day.[*]

21 Yes, they knew about him all right, but they wouldn't admit it or worship him or even thank him for all his daily care. And after a while they began to think up silly ideas of what God was like and what he wanted them to do. The result was that their foolish minds became dark and confused.

22 Claiming themselves to be wise without God, they became utter fools instead.

23 And then, instead of worshiping the glorious, ever-living God, they took wood and stone and made idols for themselves, carving them to look like mere birds and animals and snakes and puny[*] men.

24 So God let them go ahead into every sort of sex sin, and do whatever they wanted to—yes, vile and sinful things with each other's bodies.

25 Instead of believing what they knew was the truth about God, they deliberately chose to believe lies. So they prayed to the things God made, but wouldn't obey the blessed God who made these things.

26 That is why God let go of them and let them do all these evil things, so that even their women turned against God's natural plan for them and indulged in sex sin with each other.

27 And the men, instead of having normal sex relationships with women, burned with lust for each other, men doing shameful things with other men and, as a result, getting paid within their own souls with the penalty they so richly deserved.

28 So it was that when they gave God up and would not even acknowledge him, God gave them up to doing everything their evil minds could think of.

29 Their lives became full of every kind of wickedness and sin, of greed and hate, envy, murder, fighting, lying, bitterness, and gossip.

30 They were backbiters, haters of God, insolent, proud, braggarts, always thinking of new ways of sinning and continually being disobedient to their parents.

31 They tried to misunderstand,[*] broke their promises, and were heartless—without pity.

32 They were fully aware of God's death penalty for these crimes, yet they went right ahead and did them anyway and encouraged others to do them, too.

(Inc. Tyndale House Publishers. The Living Bible . Tyndale House Publishers. Kindle Edition).

21. Christian Schools teach students the truth about <u>America's Founding Fathers and America's Christian Heritage.</u>

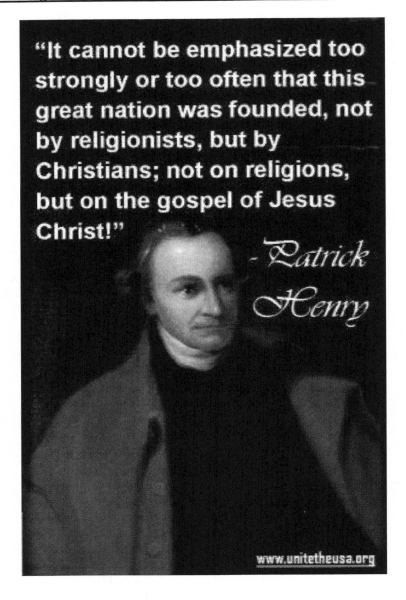

22. Christian Schools teach students that the <u>Scientific Accuracy</u> of the Bible.

We recommend reading three books public school students will probably never see.

1. **The Biblical Basis for Modern Science** by the late Dr. Henry Morris,

2. **None of these Diseases** by Dr. S.I. McMillan (MD). Dr. McMillian states that Modern Science is 4,000 years behind the Scriptures.

3. **Wilmington's Guide to the Bible** by Dr. Harold Wilmington.

Dr. Wilmington devotes nearly five pages (815-819) to this. Here are some of the scientific facts revealed in the Bible before they were "discovered" by modern science.

- *The earth is spherical (Isaiah 40:22)*

- *The earth is suspended in space (Job 26:7).*

- *Canyons & Mountains in the sea (2 Samuel 22:16) (Jonah 2:6).*

- *Springs and fountains in the oceans (Genesis 7:11) (Genesis 8:2) (Proverbs 8:28).*

- *Watery paths in the oceans (Psalm 8:8).*

- *Living things reproduce after their kind (Genesis 1:21) (Genesis 6:19).*

- Laws of health and sanitation (see page 816 in Wilmington's Guide to the Bible and page 11-13 and None of These Diseases by Dr. S. I. McMillan.

- Facts concerning the human blood stream. (Leviticus 17:11) page 817 in Wilmington's Guide to the Bible.

Another fascinating book is Dr. Henry Morris' book of Job. Dr. Morris maintains that Job is a book of science, not a book about suffering. He gives several examples. The hydrologic cycle: precipitation, evaporation, cloud construction, and the movement of moisture by wind currents. (Job 26:8) (Job 36:27, 36:28) (Job 37:16) (38:25-27) (Psalm 135:7) (Ecclesiastes 1:6,7).

23. Christian Schools teach students how to Set Reasonable Goals and Learn how to Work.

24. Christian Schools help parents Obey Deuteronomy 6:5-12

In Matthew 22: 36-40, the Pharisees asked Jesus what was the great commandment. When He answered them, Jesus quoted verse 5 from Deuteronomy 6.

5 You must love him with all your heart, soul, and might.

6 And you must think constantly about these commandments I am giving you today.

7 You must teach them to your children and talk about them when you are at home or out for a walk; at bedtime and the first thing in the morning.

8 Tie them on your finger, wear them on your forehead,

9 and write them on the doorposts of your house!"

Question: Can you really do this by taking your children to church an hour or two each week while they spend more than thirty hours every week being indoctrinated in humanism (atheism, evolution, immorality, etc.)?

25. Christian Schools help parents <u>Obey Jeremiah 10:2</u>. *"This saith the Lord, Learn not the way of the heathen. "*

26. Christian Schools help parents <u>Obey Romans 16:19</u>. *"I would have you wise unto that which is good, and simple concerning evil."*

27. Christian Schools help parents <u>Obey Proverbs 19:27</u>. *"Cease my son to hear the instruction that causeth thee to err from the words of knowledge."*

Where do we find God's words of knowledge? We find them in the Bible and the Bible is not allowed in public schools. Students in public schools spend twelve years learning things that cause them to err from the words of knowledge found in the Bible.

28. Christian Schools help parents <u>Obey Colossians 2:8</u>. *"Beware lest any man spoil you <u>through philosophy</u> and vain deceit, after <u>the tradition of men</u>, after the rudiments of the world, and not after Christ."*

29. Christian Schools help parents Obey God's Command to "Train up a child in the way he/she should go."

30. Christian Schools <u>Save Taxpayers Millions of Dollars</u> Every Year.

Our school, the Countryside Christian School of Gainesville, Florida saves taxpayers <u>$6,575.34 every day</u> for 365 days every year. How do we figure this? Every student in a public-school costs taxpayers somewhere between $8,000 and $15,000 per student every year.

Take the lowest figure ($8,000 per student). The Countryside Christian School in Gainesville has an enrolment of 300 students. 300 x $8,000 = $2,400,000.00. Divide this by 365 days in the year. That means that we save taxpayers $6,575.34 every day for 365 days every year.

In addition to that, every parent in our school pays property taxes, so we also help pay all of the expenses for every public school in Alachua County.

31. Christian Schools provide a <u>Real Education</u> rather than an <u>Indoctrination in Secular Humanism</u>.

We want to remind you again that every public school in America teaches the five lies of Secular Humanism.

"The battle for mankind's future must be waged and won in the public-school classroom by teachers who correctly perceive their role as the proselytizers of a new faith. The classroom must

and will become an arena of conflict between the old and the new. . . .the rotting corpse of Christianity and the new faith of Humanism." (Humanist, page 26 of the January/February 1983 issue).

32. Christian Schools help students <u>Remain in Church</u> and not Leave church after Graduation from High School.

The 2008 issue of Outreach Magazine featured an interesting article *titled, Don't Blame the University.* The timely article focused on the dropout rate of our young people between the ages of 18-22.

Nationally, between 70-80% of the young people in our churches will drop out of church after graduation from high school.

The dropout rate among Southern Baptist Churches is even higher than the national average. These students will leave our churches after graduation in spite of all of our emphasis on Sunday schools, educational buildings, ministers of youth, tubing and skiing parties.

33 In Christian Schools, graduation is based on <u>Work accomplished, not Birthdays</u>.

34. Christian School students can still celebrate <u>Traditional American holidays like Thanksgiving and Christmas</u>.

35. Christian Schools help churches <u>Make Better use of their Money and their Facilities</u>.

In our opinion, a church that has an understanding of the times will not spend thousands of dollars on "educational space" (Sunday school rooms) and use that space only *a few* hours every week. They might consider starting a Christian school and use that space six or seven days every week. We did and we have never regretted it.

36. In Christian Schools, parents <u>Don't Bus their Kids back to Egypt on Monday Morning</u>.

It would have been strange for Moses, after having delivered God's people out of Egypt, for him to have bussed God's children back to Egypt every Monday morning for their education?

37. Christian Schools <u>Teach Real history, not Revised History</u>.

There is a growing movement in America to turn our country into a secular state. One way to do that is to re-write history and to remove every trace of God, Christ, the Bible, and our Christian heritage from the history books. For example:

- Students are taught that Africans really discovered America by crossing the Atlantic on rafts, hundreds of years before Columbus.

- Students are taught that the ideas found in the US Constitution were really borrowed from the Iroquois Indians.

- Students are taught that the ancient Greeks and Romans stole all of their ideas from the Egyptians who were black.

- Public school students are taught that nearly everything wrong in the world today can be blamed on Columbus and the white males.

For a closer look at how history has been changed, we urge you to get a copy of this book pictured below from Amazon.com. It is available in Kindle and paperback. You can be reading the Kindle version in five minutes on your iphone, computer or ipad.

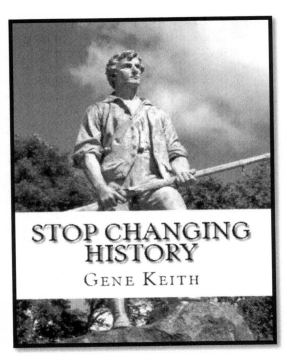

38. Christian Schools Prepare students for College and Leadership.

Lisa (Taylor) Munyon

Lisa completed the ACE curriculum at Countryside Christian School in Gainesville, Florida. She then completed both the University of Florida and Law school in five years. Lisa now serves as a Circuit Court Judge in Orlando, Florida. She has also chaired a major State-wide Supreme Court Commission for several years.

Toyna Young

Our first African-American graduate, Toyna Young, has her own law firm in Orlando, Florida. She attended the University of Florida and attended Law school in Paris. Look her up on Google.

Robby Pruitt

In 2007, another CCS graduate was named as one of the twelve greatest coaches in State History by the Florida High School Athletic Association. Robby has won more state championships than any coach in Florida High School History. Look him up on Google.

Sophia Fanelli

Sophia was also dual enrolled at SFCC. When she received her diploma from Countryside Christian School in May 2013, she already had a 4.0 record at Santa Fe College. During that time, she was also active in the sports program at Countryside.

Sophia is now working on her Masters' degree at the University of Florida. If you want your child to receive a real education, you must enrol them in a Christian school or teach them at home. There are no other options.

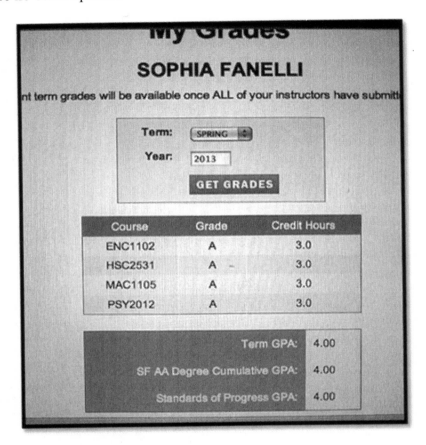

39. Christian Schools often help students <u>Find the right Husband or Wife</u>.

Our youngest son, Stevie Keith, met his wife Celesia, while attending the Countryside Christian School in Gainesville.

Rock & Michelle Meeks met while they were students at CCS. Michelle won a four-year softball scholarship to the University of Houston in Texas. Her husband, Rock, is now a County Commissioner in Levy County, Florida.

Other couples who met while attending Countryside Christian School are: Pat & Tina Robbins, Timothy & Dawn Campbell, Tex & Marsha Robertson, Tim &Terrie Williams, Steve & Beth Keene, and Nelson & Jessica Nguyen.

40. Christian School Students <u>Hear the Truths of the Bible Shared Every Week</u>.

Our three Christian Schools have chapel services every week where students are exposed to Bible preaching. This is not allowed in government schools.

41. Christian Schools teach students the <u>Truth about the Pilgrims and America's Christian Legacy</u>.

I was taught in public school that the Pilgrims were a very religious people who came to America to escape persecution and to find a place where they could bring their children up in the nurture and admonition of the Lord.

Humanists, who are revising American History books, don't like students to read the Mayflower Compact and learn about the Pilgrims. Read the first lines and you will understand why: Here are the exact words:

"In the Name of God Amen! Having undertaken for the glory of God and the advancement of the Christian faith, and honour of king and country, a voyage to plant the first colony in the Northern parts of Virginia."

- Students today are taught that the Pilgrims were a bunch of religious fanatics who couldn't get along with anybody.

- Students today are told the Pilgrims got on a ship, lost their way, and when they landed they didn't know where they were.

- Public school students are told the Pilgrims would have starved to death if it wasn't for the Indians, and Thanksgiving was a day the Pilgrims thanked the Indians for saving their lives.

- Modern public-school textbooks teach, that in return for all the Indians did for the Pilgrims, the Pilgrims brought diseases like syphilis that eventually spoiled the paradise the Indians enjoyed.

42. Christian Schools teach students the <u>Truth about the Future from the Bible</u> without the use of Crystal Balls.

Public school students never hear the truth about the Second Coming of Christ, the Great Tribulation, the coming one world government and the Anti-Christ. To make matters worse, even if they attend church, they probably never hear those things from their pulpits.

43. Christian Schools <u>Produce Leaders instead of Snowflakes</u>.

- **Tex Robertson** started out as a high school monitor in our school. He is now the Resource Manager of the Bible Broadcasting Network in Charlotte, North Carolina.

- **Pat Robbins** is a small business owner.

- **Rock Meeks** is now a County Commissioner in Levy County.

- **Lisa Taylor Munyon** is a Circuit Court Judge in Orange County, Florida.

- **Tim Williams** is a pastor and the Assistant Supervisor of Elections in Alachua County, Florida.

- Many of our graduates are teachers and principals. Many are successful parents.

- **Wade "Bubba" Townsend** is a popular dentist in Gainesville, Florida.

- **Robby Pruitt** is a successful coach and his teams have won more State Championship Games than any coach in Florida high school history.

- Our granddaughter, **Rebekka (Keene) Wade** is the Vice President and Chief Operations Officer of the Tallahassee Museum. She served as the Director of Finance for four years prior to her promotion. The Tallahassee museum is one of Florida's leading museums.

44. Christian Schools teach students the <u>Truth about Islam</u> and their plan to <u>conquer the world for Allah</u> and establish Sharia Law.

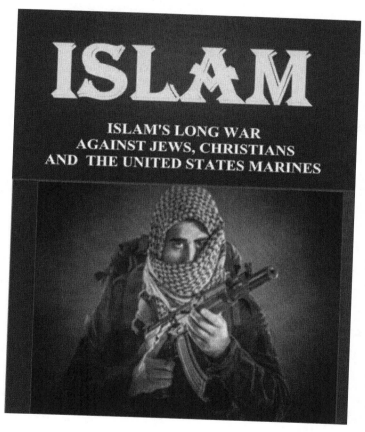

Some have predicted that if the present trends continue, the USA is on track to become a Muslim nation between 2021 and 2035, perhaps sooner. Islamic terrorists have promised to have an ISIS flag flying over the White House in this generation. Islamic terrorists plan for the United States to become can Islamic caliphate. Consider what the terrorist leaders said about their plans to turn America into an Islamic state. They are serious!

"Thanks to your democratic laws we will invade you!"

"Thanks to your religious laws we will dominate you!"

"America will have a Muslim president by the year 2020!"

Students in public schools will never be exposed to the truth about Islam. In some schools, the students. even dress in Muslim clothing.

Muslims and Christians do not worship the same God. Christians and Jews worship Jehovah, the Creator of heaven and earth. Muslims worship Allah, the sun god of the ancient Arabians.

45. Christian Schools teach students the Truth about Slavery.

"In 1860, the year before the Civil War, no Republican owned a slave. All the four million slaves at the time were owned by Democrats. Now this generalization could easily be refuted by someone providing a list of Republicans who owned slaves. The Left couldn't do it.

One assiduous researcher finally sought to dispute me with a single counter example. Ulysses S. Grant, he pointed out, once inherited a slave from his wife's family. I conceded the point but reminded him that, at the time, Ulysses S. Grant was not a Republican."*(D'Souza, Dinesh. The Big Lie: Exposing the Nazi Roots of the American Left (Kindle Locations 115-119). Regnery Publishing. Kindle Edition).*

Very few people understand how the slave trade actually worked. The first step in the story of slavery in America began when *African chiefs* raided *African villages* of other tribes and captured their *fellow Africans*.

The second step was when those African chiefs then sold those captured Africans from other villages to Arab slave traders who then moved the slaves down to the coast where they were loaded onto Dutch, English, and Portuguese ships.

At least 10 million Africans were forcibly brought to the Americas. About 47 percent of them to the Caribbean Islands and the Guianas, 38 percent went to Brazil, and only 6 percent came to mainland Spanish America.

In spite of the fact that the United Nations declared, in 1951, that the practice of slavery was declining in the world, slavery is still going on in Africa itself. Slavery is still practiced in Muslim controlled countries today.

46. Christian Schools teach students the truth about <u>America being a Republic and not a Democracy.</u>

There are scores of men and women holding public office today who actually believe the United States is a democracy. America is not a democracy. America is a Constitutional Republic.

In fact, as far as we know, the word "democracy" doesn't even appear in any of the founding documents (Declaration of Independence, The U.S. Constitution, and the Bill of Rights).

Can you recite the Pledge of Allegiance? What does it say? *"to the Republic* for which it stands, or *to the Democracy* for which it stands?

Read Article V, Section 4 of the U.S. Constitution. *"The United States shall guarantee to every state in the union a Republican form of government."*

47. Christian Schools teach students to <u>Respect Authority</u>.

Students are taught to say "Yes sir" and Yes ma'am" to adults. Our boys are taught to open the door for ladies and to respect adults. They respect their teachers, our police officers, and all who are in authority. Read Romans 13.

48. Christian Schools teach students the History of our <u>National Anthem</u>. <u>They pledge allegiance to our flag every day</u>.

49. Christian Schools teach students to <u>Respect Police and Law Enforcement Officers</u>.

In Memory of
Sgt Noel Ramirez
and
Deputy Taylor Lindsey
End of Watch: April 19, 2018

50. Christian Schools teach students the Dangers of <u>Illegal Immigration and Sanctuary Cities</u>.

51. Christian Schools learn the truth about the <u>Second Amendment</u>.

Gun control is one of the most important issues of the 21st century. Throughout history, millions of people have been murdered by their own governments, who first rendered them helpless by restricting or confiscating their firearms.

The long-range objective of the gun-control crowd is to repeal the Second Amendment and to totally disarm the citizens of this country and leave them helpless with no way to defend themselves.

The *right* to keep and bear arms is not a right granted to us by our government. It is a *God-given right*. Americans enjoyed the right to keep and bear arms before we created our government.

It is our prayer that serious, freedom-loving Americans will get their heads out the sand and refuse to be deceived by all the anti-gun propaganda. They must stand up and be counted. The right to keep and bear arms is a matter of life and death for Americans today.

52. Most Christian Schools are <u>Safer than Public Schools</u>.

53. Christian Schools teach Students <u>Why we should Support Israel</u>.

It is amazing to see how many major denominations have turned against Israel. Look them up on Google. While you are at it, read the promises and warnings in the Bible to those who turn against Israel.

54. Christian Schools teach students the <u>Dangers of Drinking Alcoholic Beverages</u>.

Students in Christian schools are allowed to read the Scriptures which explain why God created intoxicating beverages and the reasons why serious Christians should abstain.

55. Christian Schools teach the truth about <u>Mixed Marriages</u>.

This has nothing to do with race. This is about saved people marrying lost people. **Read II Corinthians 6:14-18.**

56. Christians Schools <u>oppose Racism</u> and teach students that <u>ALL Lives Matter</u>.

How many students today know that Moses' wife was black? How many students today know that the first man to carry a cross for Jesus was a black man from Cyrene, North Africa. Students in Christian Schools are taught to love and respect all people.

57. Christian School are free to teach students the part Christians played in American History and Government.

When I ran for the office of State Senate in 1980, a cry was heard from the media, the liberal establishment, and even from the churches. They would say: "You can't mix religion and politics," and "preachers have no business in politics!" People who say such things are ignorant of the Scriptures and of American history. How many public-school teachers today know the following?

Roger Williams

The first community on American soil to grant complete religious freedom to everybody was established by a Baptist preacher. The Rev. Roger Williams didn't steal land from the Native Americans. He purchased it and established Providence, Rhode Island, which was the first community on American soil in which everyone enjoyed religious freedom.

John Witherspoon

The Rev. John Witherspoon was involved in education and politics. He served as the President of Princeton, signed the Declaration of Independence, and personally trained one president, one Vice-president, three Supreme Court Justices, ten cabinet members. twelve governors, and sixty members of the U.S. Congress. This "preacher in politics" also trained another young man who had planned to enter the ministry but entered politics instead. His name was James Madison.

James Garfield

Those critics of "preachers in politics" may not know that President Garfield was also a lay preacher.

Preachers in Congress

Two pastors, Joseph Huntington and Joseph McKean, both served as presidents of the Continental Congress.

Rev. John Wise

Rev. John Wise is called "The Father of American Independence, "because of an essay he wrote which became the guide for the Declaration of Independence?

Rev. Hooker

Another "Preacher in Politics" was Rev. Hooker. He is called "The Father of American Democracy" because he wrote the Fundamental Orders of Connecticut which served as the forerunner of the U.S. Constitution.

Rev. Nathaniel Ward

The Rev. Nathaniel Ward wrote the *Massachusetts Body of Liberties*, which became the guide to the Bill of Rights.

Rev. John Leland

Much of the credit for the First Amendment to the United States Constitution goes to the Rev. John Leland of Orange County, Virginia. A monument still stands in the park there marking the spot where Rev. Leland and James Madison made an agreement that resulted in the First Amendment being added to the U.S. Constitution.

General Eisenhower

The late General Dwight D. Eisenhower, who later became President of the United States, recognized America's religious heritage. He said:

"Without God, of course, there could be no American form of government or any American way of life. Recognition of the Supreme Being is the first and most basic expression of Americanism. Thus, the founding fathers saw it, and thus with God's help it will continue to be." (Thomas Bailey, *"Trails in Florida Education,"* Tallahassee: 1963, page 103.)

Students in our public schools are not allowed to hear anything like this. If they did, the ACLU would have them in court immediately.

58. Christian Schools teach <u>Why America and Western Culture is Great</u>.

Christian schools teach individualism, free-enterprise, and love of country. Our position will probably be labelled as "hate speech" by the snowflakes and liberals. today. But we will tell the truth and let them get their crayons and hide in some safe place.

Blame America First

There is a war on   Western Culture and it is spawned on the campuses of our public schools and colleges. Multiculturalism does not allow us to teach that the American culture is superior. We can't even teach that the American culture is good.

Multiculturalists teach our children that America's injustices so far outweigh her virtues that we shouldn't even mention America's virtues.

Some students today have been led to believe that the American flag itself is racist. God help us!

The Secret of the Greatness of Western Culture
Acts 16 (Living Bible)

1 Paul and Silas went first to Derbe and then on to Lystra where they met Timothy, a believer whose mother was a Christian Jewess, but his father a Greek.

2 Timothy was well thought of by the brothers in Lystra and Iconium,

3 so Paul asked him to join them on their journey. In deference to the Jews of the area, he circumcised Timothy before they left, for everyone knew that his father was a Greek and hadn't permitted this before.[*]

4 Then they went from city to city, making known the decision concerning the Gentiles, as decided by the apostles and elders in Jerusalem.

5 So the church grew daily in faith and numbers.

Paul Wanted to Go East. The Holy Spirit Said No!

6 Next they traveled through Phrygia and Galatia because the Holy Spirit had told them not to go into the Turkish province of Asia Minor at that time.

7 Then going along the borders of Mysia they headed north for the province of Bithynia, but again the Spirit of Jesus said no.

8 So instead they went on through Mysia province to the city of Troas.

God Sent Paul's West

9 That night[*] Paul had a vision. In his dream he saw a man over in Macedonia, Greece, pleading with him, "Come over here and help us."

10 Well, that settled it. We [*] would go to Macedonia, for we could only conclude that God was sending us to preach the Good News there.

Let This Sink In

Paul, Silas and Timothy set out on a missionary journey from the main church. They planned to travel toward the east, but the Holy Spirit stopped them twice. Then Paul had the dream about the man over in Greece crying out for help (verse 9). That is when Paul decided to take the Gospel to the west rather than the east.

I am so glad he did. That is why Western Culture became so far advanced over the east. In fact, today, those in the east still worship animals and where false religion and paganism abounds.

59. ACE Schools used the <u>Five Laws of Learning</u> which places them "light years" ahead of all Government Schools.

How many public-school administers or teachers do you know who are even familiar with the Five Laws of Learning.

Law 1: Students must be on a <u>level of curriculum</u> where they can perform. Chronological age only tells you when a student is born. 1

113

Law 2: Students must <u>set goals</u> that can be achieved in a prescribed period of time.

Law 3: Students must be <u>controlled and motivated</u> so they can achieve, assimilate, and use the material.

Law 4: Students achievement <u>must be measurable</u>.

Law 5: Students achievement <u>must be rewarded</u>.

Please go on line and follow the following link. The video will go into detail and explain the Five Laws of Learning. **Http://youtu.be/qrQQIz6CEZ8**

60. Nowhere in the Bible does God give His people permission to allow their children to be educated by unbelievers. On the contrary, the Scriptures abound with prohibitions against it.

Summary

The public school is an experiment that has failed. To make matters worse, the public -school system is probably the most destructive influence on American culture in the world today. It is a union-controlled, politically protected monopoly that is hostile, not only to God, Jesus Christ, and the Bible in general, but to Western values and culture in particular. One hope for the preservation of our Republic is to train a new generation of freedom loving Americans to help turn this nation back to God and restore our God-given freedoms guaranteed in the Bill of Rights. The only choices are to home school, or to enrol your children in a Christian School.

CHAPTER 10

Does it Really Matter Where Your Children Attend School?

1. Does it matter whether children get an education rather than an indoctrination?

2. Does it matter whether children are taught the truth about God, evolution, morality, and a socialist one-world government?

3. Does it matter that more than 80% of the youth in our churches will leave church after graduation and never return?

4. Does it matter to you that the five lies of secular humanism are taught in every public school in America?

5. Do you really understand humanism?

We suggest parents and especially pastors, read two of Tim LaHayes' books, **"The Battle for the Mind, "**and *"***The Battle for the Public Schools."**These books should be required reading for everyone in the ministry. I would call these books "Humanism 101."

6. Does it matter that parents who allow their children to attend public school are disobeying Jeremiah 10:2? *"This saith the Lord, Learn not the way of the heathen.*

7. Does it matter that parents who allow their children to attend public school are disobeying Proverbs 19:27? *"Cease my son to hear the instruction that causeth thee to err from the words of knowledge."*

Is it even remotely possible for a student to attend a public school and not hear things that cause them to turn away from God, Christianity and the Bible?

They hear those things every day. When our children receive a diploma from a public school, they have spent 15,120 hours ignoring and disobeying this clear command in Proverbs 19:27. What part of cease to hear do we not understand?

8. Can a Christian parent allow their child to attend a public school and not violate Colossians 2:8? *"Beware lest any man spoil you through philosophy and vain deceit, after the tradition of men, after the rudiments of the world, and not after Christ."*

Every student who attends a public school must reject most of what he/she learns there, or they will have been "spoiled" or taken captive by the philosophy and religion of humanism.

9. Can a Christian parent allow their child to attend a Public School and not disobey what God commanded in Romans 16:19? *"I would have you wise unto that which is good, and simple concerning evil."*

What does it mean to be "simple concerning evil?" Where are our children exposed to all sorts of evil today? The answer is obvious. In our opinion, the public schools have done more harm to this nation than any other influence in the history of this republic.

10. Does your pastor believe your children should attend a public school?

11. What Possible Reason (or excuse) can you really give for allowing your children to attend a Public School?

Nowhere in the Bible does God give His people permission to allow their children to be educated by unbelievers. On the contrary, the Scriptures abound with prohibitions against it.

To make matters worse, the public -school system is probably the most destructive influence on American culture in the world today. It is a union-controlled, politically protected monopoly that is hostile, not only to God, Jesus Christ, and the Bible in general, but to Western values and culture in particular.

The *philosophy* of all public (government) schools is wrong!

118

The *curriculum* in government schools is wrong!

The *peer pressure* in government schools is often wrong!

The *sex education* in government schools is definitely wrong!

Our Challenge

One hope for the preservation of our republic is to train a new generation of freedom loving Americans to help turn this nation back to God and restore our God-given freedoms guaranteed in the Bill of Rights.

The only choices are to home school, or to enrol your children in a Christian school. In our opinion, it is past time for serious Christian parents to remove their children from the public school system.

We Report! You Decide!

CHAPTER 11

Countryside Christian School is Making a Difference

Countryside Christian School not only provides 300 students a quality, Christ-centered education, we also save the taxpayers of Alachua County $2,400,000.00 every year. That comes to

$46,153,84 every week, and $6,576.34 every day; for 365 days every year.

Pastors! Please pray about starting a Christian School in your church. We did that forty-five years ago, and it was one of the wisest decisions we have ever made. Here is how it happened.

Back on 1974, God gave the Southside Baptist Church of Gainesville, Florida a bold vision. God clearly led our congregation to no longer be satisfied with a traditional week end ministry. We were troubled that our public-school system was not only becoming more hostile to Christians every day, it was beginning to fail academically as well. They not only had removed God, prayer, and the Bible from the classroom, they had actually become openly hostile to believers.

The Purpose of Public Schools

As we have mentioned several times already, we finally understood that the purpose of our public schools had changed when we read the following remarks by Chester Pierce, professor of educational psychiatry at Harvard University, given at a childhood education seminar in 1973.

"Every child in America entering school at the age of five is mentally ill, because he comes to school with certain allegiances toward our founding fathers, toward our elected officials, toward his parents, toward a belief in a supernatural Being, toward the sovereignty of this nation as a separate entity. It's up to you teachers to make all of these sick children well by creating the international child of the future."

80 % of Youth Leave Church After Graduation

We were not aware back in 1974 that more than 80 percent of the young people attending Southern Baptist Churches and public schools leave church after graduation and never return. It doesn't take a rocket scientist to understand why.

1,872 Hours Spent in Church

Students spend a maximum of 156 hours a year in church (if they are never absent). 3 hours x 52 weeks = 156 hours per year in church. They spend 156 hours per year x 12 years = 1,872 hours in church by the time they graduate from high school.

15,120 Hours Spent in Public School

During that same time, they spend 7 hours per day for 5 days every week in public school. This is to total of 35 hours every week. They spend 180 days every year in public school. This means 7 hours per day for 180 days = 1,260 hours per year being indoctrinated in humanism.

Students spend 12 years (not including Kindergarten) before graduation. This is 1,260 hours x 12 years = 15,120 hours by the time they graduate, where it is illegal to hear from the Bible, but where they are being indoctrinated in Humanism.

Our New Mission

We had to decide that regardless of what others said or did, we had to obey God and begin teaching our children Monday through Friday and Sundays as well. We were convinced this is our mission.

The Role of Government, the Home & the Church

We are also convinced that education is the job of the home and the church, not the government. In fact, according to the Bible and the Constitution, government has no business even meddling in education. Because of government education, we are now living in the most illiterate period in the history of this Republic.

The Bible says: "Where there is no vision, the people perish." I shared this vision for a Christian School with the congregation and they voted to follow me. That's how it all started.

Two Major Problems

Once we decided to have a Christian School we had to face two problems: 1). We had no money, and 2) Nobody in our church (including the pastor) had ever attended a Christian school or knew anything about a Christian school. We all had attended public schools and none of us had even been in a Christian School. Yet, that didn't deter us. We had a bold vision. We were convinced this was God's Will and if we followed God's Will, He would keep His promise and provide all of our needs.

We Rejected Traditional Thinking

When we first began planning a Christian school we thought like most other churches thought. We would begin with a daycare, add a kindergarten, and then add a grade a year until one day we would have a full school with grades K-12.

God's Clear Leadership

This is where God began to give us very clear leadership. The Lord convinced us that we were not going the traditional route. We were going to start a school with grades 2-12 the very first year.

How would we do that? We had no idea, but we were convinced that this was God's specific will. In addition to that, this present writer had three sons who were still in grades nine, ten, and eleven in public school, and he was not going to leave them out. To make matters even more difficult, two of our boys played football for a very popular school and their coach did not like the idea of losing them at all. I am so thankful that none of our sons were rebellious and none of them resisted our transferring them to a small new school with no sports program at that time.

No Previous Experience

As we stated previously, none of us had ever attended a Christian School so we decided to visit some schools. The first school we were led to visit was the large North Florida Christian School in Tallahassee, Florida. We had met the pastor, so we made an appointment, traveled to Tallahassee, and spent the day with the principal, visiting the school and gathering information. When we returned home, we were convinced that this was the model we would follow.

Accelerated Christian Education

About that time, we received a call from another pastor friend of mine who was the pastor of the First Baptist Church of Mims, Florida. This pastor had recently started a different kind of school, which we had never heard of, nor were we really interested in that idea. However, since we were friends and we didn't want to offend him, we agreed to at least visit their school. Actually, I didn't visit the school myself, but asked our Associate Pastor, Keith Spurgers and his wife Pauline, to go spend the day down at Mims, to check this new kind of school out. To be perfectly honest, both of us were very sceptical and they actually went down to Mims looking for faults.

Thanks to Keith and Pauline Spurgers

When Brother Keith Spurgers, and his wife, Pauline, returned, their evaluation startled us. He went down to Mims a sceptic and returned convinced that this was the kind of school we should build. He was sold on Accelerated Christian Education (ACE). I trusted Brother Spurgers judgment and from that moment on, we decided t go with ACE.

First Big Test – No Money

The first big test we faced was the $1000 to enter into a contract with Accelerated Christian Education in Lewisville, Texas, and the money for Tuelah and I to fly out to Texas for a week. God supplied that need in an unexpected way. One of our radio listeners from Ft. McCoy sent us a check for $1,000. We did not ask for the check, but she had felt led of God to send it. It arrived just in time. As far as the air-fare to Texas, we had saved up our next month's house payment and used that to pay for the air travel. It might be interesting to know that the lady from Ft. McCoy who sent the check became one of our first school monitors.

Second Test - No Teachers

When we finally decided to start a Christian School, I was in for a very unpleasant surprise. I knew quite a few certified Christian teachers over in Levy County who were then teaching in public schools. Those teachers had been teenagers when I was a pastor in Otter Creek and I assumed they would be standing in line for a chance to serve God in a Christian school. I was in for the surprise of my life. Not one of those teachers was willing to leave the money and benefits of the public school.

The very last Christian teacher I had called made an appointment for an interview. When she didn't show up for the interview I called her and asked her why? She replied that she had talked to her pastor and that her pastor had advised her not to leave the public school with its pay and benefits and teach in a Christian School. I was so disappointed. This man was a friend of mine and a pastor in the Harmony Baptist Association.

Third Test - Parents' Question

Bear in mind that I am a pastor who had never attended a Christian School, starting a new Christian School in September, with grades 2-12, down in "Porter's Quarters" in Gainesville, Florida.

We followed the prescribed procedures and interviewed each prospective parent and each prospective student. During those interviews, each parent wisely asked us: *"Are your teachers certified?"*

To which I honestly answered: *"To be perfectly honest with you, we don't have the first teacher yet. But God is going to provide them."*

Would you believe that not one parent backed out. They would sit there and look at me for a moment, and then say, *"I believe God will provide them,"* and signed their enrolment application.

That experience made a deep impression on me. I promised God that since those parents had placed so much trust in me, I would rather die than to let them down.

Fourth Test - Back Surgery

Try to remember that this is the summer of 1974 and we are opening a new school with grades 2-12 in September and we still don't have the first teacher. About that time, I had a serious back injury and the pain was unbearable. We lived in McIntosh, Florida, on Orange Lake, and to be able to endure the pain as we drove to work each day, my wife, Tuelah would drive and I would curl up in fatal position on the back seat. Finally, we realized that surgery was unavoidable.

A Major Test of Faith

It is now June and our new school opens in September with grades 2-12, and we still had not hired the first teacher. I had major back surgery on Thursday, went home on Saturday in a pickup truck, and was told to remain in bed one week. I have not had one pain since I woke up from surgery and didn't have to take even one pain pill the entire time.

God Miraculously Provided Teachers

During that week, while lying in bed recovering from back surgery, looking out on Orange Lake through my bedroom window, God brought our new teachers to me for their interviews. I hired our entire staff while lying in bed recovering from back surgery.

God Miraculously Provided the Students

God was teaching me a valuable lesson. When we first began planning our school, we had hoped to enrol approximately 40 students, grades 2-12. We were surprised and thrilled to have 80 students in grades 2-12 our very first year.

God Miraculously Provided the Classrooms

The school grew rapidly, and the second year, Kindergarten and First Grades were added. Soon, the entire church facility, including the auditorium was then converted into to a High School Learning Center.

Rented Public School for Sunday Meetings

At that time, the church began renting different places to meet on Sundays and Wednesday nights. The church met for a time at the old Kirby Smith School and then moved to the Women's Club on West University Avenue, where we met until we moved into the present facilities on 39th Avenue.

Gainesville Was Moving West

As our church and school grew we began to look for property on the west side of town. We had read a survey by Bell Telephone Company that one day the center of Gainesville would possibly be near I-75. We began to look for land and found 6.5 acres on Tower Road, raised the money and paid cash for it.

We had plans drawn for a building when God led us to stop. The Lord revealed to us that, if we built on Tower Road we would soon be overcrowded like we were in southeast Gainesville. After much prayer, we put everything on hold and began to pray and look for a larger tract of land for our church and school.

Fifth Test - Needed More Room Again

In 1977, with the help of Mr. Jake Perry and the local Agriculture Agent, the church found the present forty-acre site on N.W. 39th Avenue. There were three problems in this phase.

1. The land was not for sale.

2. If they did sell the land, they definitely would not sell just 10 acres we had asked for.

3. The church didn't have any money.

After much prayer, the owner of the land agreed to sell the land, if we would take the entire 40 acres and build a school. The church immediately began to look for funds. After inquiring at several institutions, First Federal of Gainesville agreed to loan the church the necessary funds and the land was purchased. This, by the way, is the second time the church has ever borrowed money.

We Sold the Church in Porter's Quarters

Eventually, Alachua County purchased our original church property on S.W. Second Terrace and the proceeds from that sale were used to purchase and construct the two large metal buildings on the present forty-acre site. The two buildings are identical and were originally designed to be used for school classrooms. Although one building is now used as an auditorium, the plumbing is already installed beneath the floor of the church auditorium for convenient conversion to future classrooms, restrooms, and showers.

Later, the 6.5 acres we owned on Tower Road were sold and the proceeds from that sale were used to completely retire the debt on the 40 acres.

Countryside Christian Church & School 2019

Christian Education is a priority at Countryside Christian School. We have had a Christian school with grades K-12 since 1974. Our church is now located on a beautiful forty-acre campus just West of I-75. We moved here from S.E. Gainesville in 1977. At the present time we are enjoying our brand new, multi-purpose building with a large gymnasium, new classrooms, and a modern kitchen. We have 300 students and a full-time staff of 45 people. We also have a school in Gilchrist County named Riverside Christian School.

Gene Keith - First Pastor, Principal & Coach
Tuelah Keith - First School Secretary

Second Principal Jerry Milton & His wife Norma

Third Principal Bill Keith & His Wife Vonnie

Fourth Principal David Keith & His Wife Sherri

Present Principal Jody Robertson & His Wife Jessica

School Secretary Natalie Wilson

Secretary Faith Myers

Minister of Finance & Office Manager Jessica Robertson

Countryside Staff

New All Purpose Building

God is Good - All the Time!

Countryside Christian Minutemen

Volleyball

2019 FCAL South Division Champs

Softball

Boys Basketball Team & Cheer Leaders

Football

Annual Beast Feast

Archery

Faithful Fans

Awards Presentation

Dinner on the Grounds

CHAPTER 12

Riverside Christian School is Making a Difference

Riverside Christian School not only provides 125 students with a Christ-centered quality education, they save taxpayers $1,000,000.00 every year. That averages $19,230.76 every week for 52 weeks every year.

How it All Began

In 2007, The Trustees of the Suwannee Valley Christian Academy voted to give their school building and property to the

Countryside Baptist Church of Gainesville, Florida. We reorganized the school and began with forty students in grades K through twelve.

Mrs. Gwen Keith, who had taught in the Countryside Christian School for more than twenty years, became the Principal. The Suwannee Valley Christian Academy was renamed the Riverside Christian School.

The school presently has 125 students and a brand new building, a gymnasium, and a sports complex. One family donated the money to build the new building, and again, praise God, RCS is debt free.

Principal Gwen Keith

Secretary Ginger Russell

2018 Riverside Staff

Riverside Christian 2017 FCAL Champions

2018 FCAL Football Champions

Riverside Christian School is Making a Difference

CHAPTER 13

Creekside Christian School is Making a Difference

Creekside Christian School not only provides a quality education for 100 students, five days every week. They save taxpayers $800,000.00 ever year. That averages $15,384.00 every week for 52 weeks every year.

Our son, Bill Keith. attended the old Otter Creek Public School (now the Lark building) when he was a child. In those days the school only went to the sixth grade. After that all the students were bussed to Bronson, Florida.

Bill later became the pastor of the Otter Creek Church and had a vision for a truly Christian School. After much prayer, hard work, and perseverance, the church opened a new school with grades K through 12. The school is still going strong and our Granddaughter, Mrs. Ginny (Yearty) Keith serves as the Principal.

Let Pastor Bill Keith Tell the Story

The picture below is Bill Keith, the founder of the school, and his daughter-in-law- Ginny (Yearty) Keith, who is the principal of the school, and Bill's granddaughter, Emma Grace, who graduated from Creekside Christian School.

My first church experience of church and hearing the sweet stories of Jesus was at Otter Creek Baptist Church. I remember Sunday school there as a small child of three or four with kind ladies teaching me about Jesus and the other great Bible heroes!

It wasn't hard for me to come back there 35 years later and become the pastor of that wonderful little church on the edge of the wilderness that is Gulf Hammock. Some of those kind ladies were still alive when my wife and I arrived back home there in 1992.

Little did we know at the time, but God had great plans in store for this out-of-the-way church on the edge of nowhere!

I attended public school for the first two years of my education at the Otter Creek (public) School that held classes for the first through sixth grades.

The old school closed after the integration of the 1960s. It was reopened sometime in the late 70s for a day training center for the Levy Association of Retarded Citizens and is still in operation as such to this day. The old building still brings back good memories of my childhood when starting school there so long ago.

God Had Special Plans

I never planned to move back to Otter Creek and become the Pastor of the church there as I was very busy in ministry in my home church, the Countryside Baptist in Gainesville.

The opportunity came to me while on a hunting trip down in that area during the fall of 1992. Sammy Yearty, a family friend who was also Chairman of the Deacon Board there at Otter Creek Baptist, approached me as I was leaving the hunting woods one

Saturday afternoon and heading home. He asked if I would pray about coming down and serving as their interim pastor until they could call a full time one. I told him that I would certainly pray about that.

I was then serving as the Principal of Countryside Christian School, as well as Visitation pastor, Staff Counsellor, Song Leader, and Sunday school teacher for the Countryside Baptist Church where my father served as Senior Pastor.

I brought the idea before the men of Countryside and they agreed that God was leading me in that direction.

I accepted the call to serve as an interim pastor of Otter Creek, but still serve as Principal at Countryside Christian School. This arrangement worked out well as I would travel over to Otter Creek on Wednesday nights and Sundays for church.

We were living in Newberry at the time. It soon became evident that God had bigger plans for me at Otter Creek and soon they issued me the opportunity to become their full time Pastor, while still maintaining my other ministry as Principal at Countryside. We were offered the use of the pastorium at Otter Creek as part of our salary there and agreed to move there.

Reluctantly, we left our huge, beautiful four BR, three bath block home on five acres and moved into a small two bedroom one bath parsonage in Otter Creek. I had lived in this same small home as a young child when my father served as pastor there from 1954-1959. It hadn't changed much since that time and was quite a culture shock to my wife and children, but God had sent us there and that was where we were going to serve!

God Revealed the Need

There were many children in the Otter Creek Church and the surrounding community at the time and I soon became burdened for them as I noticed how much illiteracy abounded among their numbers! Many of them were struggling with basic reading and writing and were already in the fourth and fifth grades in the public schools there. I knew that we had the answer for this, having served as a principal for five years in a Christian School before arriving.

God Sent Help

I shared my burden with any that would listen and determined then and there to do my part to help them. I enlisted the best reading teacher we had at the time working at the Countryside Christian School. Mrs. Carole Bixby would come over on Wednesday nights and offer basic reading classes. We soon had five or six students on a regular basis with even a few adults coming to learn how to read.

Mrs. Bixby enlisted the help of her son Dale, one of our Countryside students, to come and tutor the students as well and soon many of them were making startling improvement in their reading ability. The miracle began as a Wednesday night reading class that helped plant the seeds and plough the ground that would a few years later grow into an even greater miracle!

God Gave the Pastor a Clear Vision

God began to establish a clear vision of a Christian school there at Otter Creek during these humble attempts at helping these youngsters and a few adults learn to read. I knew that a school was what the church needed and began to share the vision with others. Many Christians there caught the vision and began to change the way they viewed education, while others just wrote me off as a nut! But, God wouldn't let me forget what He wanted done there and continued to inspire my mind with the idea and plan for a Christian school at Otter Creek. I ate it, drank it, preached it, sold it, and did everything in my power to push toward starting a school there.

Refused to Split the Church

Finally, on Sept. 24, 1996, (my birthday), during a Sunday night business meeting we voted about starting a school there. The vote ended with 51% in favour and 49% against. We won the vote! Yet I felt in my heart of hearts that we should table the idea for a while and allow God to change the hearts of the other 49% before we pushed something through that might split that wonderful little church. Many of the supporters were disappointed but understood that the idea and vision was correct, the timing was just not quite there yet! So we waited on God and continued winning people to Christ and building people in the faith.

Waited on God

I put the school idea on a back burner and quit even talking about it, knowing that God was more than able to move in the hearts and minds of the people when He was ready!

My youngest daughter was the last of my three children to graduate from Countryside Christian. She finished in May of 2001. I decided that it was time to retire from being a bi-vocational pastor and devote more time to building the church there at Otter Creek.

I resigned as Principal that summer and looked forward to resting a while with just one profession and calling. I certainly wouldn't miss the 83-mile round trip every day! Little did I know that my rest would be short-lived. and God would push us forward into a great miracle! It was then that the vision of a school at Otter Creek came rushing back to me from the Lord!

God's Timing is Perfect

This time it came in the form of many of the leaders there at Otter Creek asking me when we were going to start "our school!"

The vision had grown from being something that only I was seeing to one that was embraced, cherished, and pushed by many of those I had ministered to for nine years! God had been working overtime on pushing His agenda even when I had quit speaking much about it! I was in awe of how He had done these things and the Scripture from Acts 2:17 came to mind,

"And it shall come to pass in the last days, saith God, I will pour out of my Spirit upon all flesh: and your sons and your daughters shall prophesy, and your young men shall see visions, and your old men shall dream dreams:"

Some of the young people would share with me what God was saying to them about a school. An older man there told me he had seen in a dream the school with the parking lot already partially finished! I knew then it was time to pursue the dream again!

We held a business meeting and voted the second time on whether or not to start a school there. The vote was 99% in favour. There was only one vote against! The one that cast the nay vote was older and many members thought that she didn't understand what we were even voting for!

The church fathers were still a little reluctant to take on a financial responsibility like that so it was agreed that they would allow Countryside Baptist Church to license the school and operate it there at the Otter Creek Baptist facility.

It was a partnership made in Heaven! We had the expertise on how to do it, we just needed a place to do it! Now we had that, and we made plans to open Creekside Christian School in the fall of 2001 in Otter Creek, Florida!

The Miracle on Main Street

It was a marriage made in Heaven with two churches working together to establish something there that had never happened before! It was the miracle on Main Street!

I knew that Countryside didn't have the money to fund another school, but they did have the name and backing to stand behind this new school! So I set about the task of raising the necessary $5000-$6000 start-up funds I knew we would need!

I had bought a large industrial paining machine quite by accident the year before this as a personal investment. I put a ridiculous bid of $50 on this machinery knowing that I would never get it for that price! Yet when the bids were tallied, the winning bid didn't fulfill his bid and I got the machine for $50! I immediately began to try and resell it thinking that perhaps it would provide some much -needed cash for the Keith household!

God Always Provides

It didn't sell for a long time! I advertised it all over the world on the internet, but to no avail! During the summer of 2001 a wood working shop opened in Otter Creek, 100 yards from our church door. The owner took one look at my big old machine and bought it instantly for $2,500!

I jumped up and down for joy thinking how awesome God was selling that stupid machine 100 yards from where He wanted the money used! Wow! What a sense of humour our God has!

I wrote many of my friends and family members and asked them to help! They came through in such a miraculous way and soon we had enough seed money to start the school. We still needed desks and equipment and I begin to search for those things.

A school down in Titusville had closed part of their learning centers and had enough desks and much of the curriculum that we would need to begin our school. I offered them $2500.00 for all of it and they took it! A group of wonderful men with three trucks and trailers went with me there and we brought it all back to Otter Creek the same day! We immediately began setting up the learning center and classrooms and soon our little school was within a few weeks of starting!

Over those few months in the summer of 2001, we raised somewhere close to $10,000 in start-up funding through the kindness and generosity of God's people. Some were kind enough to loan us funds over the first 5 or 6 years of the school there that made it possible to never have to ask for money or borrow from lending institutions of any kind! We were able to pay them back completely over the years and were never in debt as an institution!

Miracle After Miracle

Since that time, Creekside has experienced miracle after miracle as God provided for each and everything we would ever need to build and maintain a school! Starting with just 24 students and a vision from God we were able to establish a Christian School in Otter Creek that is still operating today. The student count now averages 75-100 each year and hundreds of boys and girls have been educated there.

Part of my family still serves there and my grandchildren are still attending school there. An added blessing is that I still get to conduct chapel in Otter Creek every Monday morning.

Countless souls have been reached for the Kingdom of God through the efforts of the dedicated teachers and staff there at Creekside. Although God called me back to my former mission at Countryside in 2010, the ministry there at Otter Creek still has a wonderful place in my heart! I am thankful for having been one of those that God used to help establish what He wanted there. I hope and pray that the ministry of Otter Creek Baptist Church and Creekside Christian School is still in operation when the Lord returns one day for His church!

Bill Keith

Creekside Christian School is Making a Difference

CHAPTER 14

Jake and Darlene Perry Have Made a Difference

I have served in the ministry for more than sixty-five years (2019) and I've never known an individual or a couple who have done more for Christian education than Jake and Darlene Perry.

Back in 1974, I was the pastor of the Southside Baptist Church of Gainesville, Florida and had a daily radio program that would be classed as "talk radio" today. One day as I was sharing my vision for a Christian School, Jake Perry was driving his tractor and listening to my daily radio show. He was a successful farmer over in Hawthorne, Florida. When he heard me sharing about our plans for a Christian School, the Holy Spirit clearly spoke to his heart. When the program was over, he went inside and told Darlene that he believed God was leading him to enrol their two children in our school.

Jake and Darlene already understood the importance of Christian education. They lived in Hawthorne and Darlene drove their two children all the way to Bellview, Florida, so they could attend a Christian School. Darlene would drive from Hawthorne to Bellview and back, twice every day. We want to mention this to emphasize the fact that this family believed in Christian Education. This was not just a preference with them. It was a conviction.

When they enrolled their daughter, Beverly and their son, Dave, in our school, Jake and Darlene went right to work and supported us beyond our wildest dreams.

When our son, Bill was called to preach and moved to Lynchburg, Virginia to attend Liberty University, Jake not only gave Bill a pick-up truck with a welding machine, Jake and Darlene also helped Bill with his college tuition.

When Jake and Darlene not only enrolled their children in our school, they began to work hard to help us improve our school. In 1977, with the help of Mr. Jake Perry and the local Agriculture Agent, the church found the present forty-acre site on N.W. 39th Avenue. As we mentioned previously, there were three problems in this phase.

1) The land was not for sale.

2) If they did sell the land, they definitely would not sell just 10 acres we had asked for.

3) We didn't have any money. For some reason, Jake continued to stop by and visit with the owners of the forty acres.

Finally, the wife, who was the actual owner of the property, told Jake that she would sell the forty acres if we would build a school on the property and not just a church. Little did she know that this was the reason we wanted the property in the first place. When we moved out to the new forty acre site, Jake brought his large tractors and other farm equipment to help begin preparing the land. Later, Jake and Darlene moved to Bronson and Darlene began helping Pastor Bill Keith build the Creekside Christian School in Otter Creek, Florida, where she is still active today (2019).

Jake and Darlene Have Made a Difference

The Author and the Editor Have Made a Difference

Gene & Tuelah Keith

True Love

"Gene Keith is part of a ten generation legacy of pioneer Christian leaders from Kentucky, Texas, and Florida. Since 1773 when John Keith hosted the first meeting of Virginia's Ten Mile Baptist Church, the Keith men for at least ten generations have led their congregations as Baptist preachers, elders or deacons, to be pioneers in sharing the Gospel.

By wagon, on horseback, on foot, and by car, they've traveled carrying the Good News of Christ from the thick forests of Virginia, across the green mountains of Kentucky, to the High Plains of Texas before finally turning back southeast to settle in sun-drenched Central Florida where three generations now pastor two churches just 20 miles apart. *"("Circling the Wagons," which appeared in the Florida Baptist Witness January 28, 2013 Joni B. Hannigan, Managing Editor).*

Gene Keith was born William Eugene Keith in Tarpon Springs, Florida, on December 25, 1932. He graduated from the Tarpon Springs High School in 1950, married his sweetheart, Tuelah Evelyn Riviere in 1952. Gene became a Christian in 1952 and entered the ministry in 1953.

Gene attended Stetson University, the University of Florida, and received his B.A. from Luther Rice University and Seminary.

He has many years of experience in the Christian School movement. He is the founder of the Countryside Christian School which celebrated its 44th Anniversary in 2018.

Gene also served as a Consultant and a Field Representative for Accelerated Christian Education, during which time he helped establish a number of Christian Schools in Florida. Many of his family are involved in education serving as Christian School `Principals and Teachers.

Gene retired in 2010 after 50 plus years in the ministry and is presently Pastor Emeritus of the Countryside Baptist Church of

Gainesville, Florida. He spends most of his time writing and speaking.

Other Books by Gene Keith

You Can Understand the Revelation.

Daniel: The Key to Prophecy

Cremation: Are You Sure?

It's All About Jesus

Religious but Lost

Suicide: Is Suicide the Unpardonable Sin?

Getting Started Right: A Handbook for Serious Christians

Easter: Facts versus Fiction

How to Enjoy Christmas in a World that has lost its Way

Evolution: Facts versus Fiction

Why do Bad Things Happen to God's People?

The Radical Same Sex Revolution

Can a Saved Person Ever be Lost Again?

Otter Creek: True Stories of People and Places

Public School or Christian School?

One Nation Under God - or Allah. Can America Survive?

Financial Solutions (A Handbook for Church Leaders)

Our Story: God is Good- - All the Time!

Stop Changing History

10 Critical Issues Christians Must Face

The Pope, Guns, Walls, & Donald Trump

If you would like to order any of Gene's books, go to Amazon.com, type in Books by Gene Keith and follow the links.

Thank you for reading this book. If you have questions or comments, you may correspond with Gene by email:**gk122532@gmail.com**.

Made in the USA
San Bernardino, CA
09 February 2019